Praise for

"While challenging biblical infamibility through engagement with their own contexts, Zilpha Elaw, Sojourner Truth, and Julia Foote left behind theological road maps for antiracist work in contemporary contexts. Kate Hanch explores these Black women's stories in her much needed and relevant work, *Storied Witness*. As a white woman who recognizes her own legacy of sin that dehumanized Black women, Hanch places front and center the narratives, sermons, and memoirs of Elaw, Truth, and Foote to argue for a Trinitarian theme of humility, embodiment, and mystic spiritualism that should move all believers to relational empathy. In a day and age when empathy is under fire, I welcome Hanch's work as another tool to fight against the callousness that seems to be overtaking present-day Christianity."

ANGELA N. PARKER, author of *If God Still Breathes, Why Can't I? Black Lives Matter and Biblical Authority* and assistant professor of New Testament and Greek, McAfee School of Theology

"Kate Hanch delivers an engaging and thoughtful reading of Elaw, Foote, and Truth. Embracing the mystical, pastoral, and prophetic elements of these Black women preachers, Hanch bravely defines them as theologians who drew on their bodily, cultural, and biblical knowledge to counter the narratives of white supremacist traditions subverting nineteenth-century Christian churches."

KIMBERLY BLOCKETT, editor of *Memoirs of the Life, Religious Experience, Ministerial Travels, and Labours of Mrs. Elaw* and professor of English, Penn State University

"How can contemporary persons of faith listen to and learn from the prophetic theologies of nineteenth-century Black women preachers in the United States? In her timely, compelling book, Kate Hanch shows how Zilpha Elaw, Julia Foote, and Sojourner Truth, each in her own way, center justice and contemplation, are led by the Holy Spirit in creative interpretations of Scripture, and provide a vision of the way of Jesus that is attentive to embodiment and materiality—dimensions that are sorely needed in our churches and society today. I plan to share this wonderful book both in the seminary classroom and in my own community of faith."

NANCY ELIZABETH BEDFORD, author of *Who Was Jesus and What Does It Mean to Follow Him?* and Georgia Harkness Professor of Theology, Garrett-Evangelical Theological Seminary

"In *Storied Witness*, Kate Hanch challenges predominant and embedded notions of theology and theologizing by examining the life and works of African American women preachers Zilpha Elaw, Julia Foote, and Sojourner Truth. In so doing, she calls for us to see Elaw, Foote, and Truth not only as nineteenth-century pioneering preachers but also as thinkers and theologians who wrestled with text and context to construct a pastoral and prophetic theology."

ANDRE E. JOHNSON, author of *No Future in This Country: The Prophetic Pessimism of Bishop Henry McNeal Turner* and associate professor of rhetoric and media studies, University of Memphis

"It was refreshing to read this work from Dr. Hanch, who writes from a different experience, yet writes as one who is compassionately interested in sharing the stories and struggles of others—specifically, of Black women preachers and theologians, who have been humiliated historically, but did not allow that to prevent them from doing their best to walk in their calling. Enjoyed this reading."

BARRY SETTLE, author of *Reset* and pastor of Allen Chapel AME Church Riverside, CA

STORIED WITNESS

STORIED WITNESS

WITNESS

The Theology of Black Women Preachers
in 19th-Century America

KATE HANCH

FORTRESS PRESS
MINNEAPOLIS

STORIED WITNESS
The Theology of Black Women Preachers in 19th-Century America

Cover image: "The Sanctuary" by Edwin Forbes, copper plate etching, 1876
Cover design: Kristin Miller

Print ISBN: 978-1-5064-8187-6
eBook ISBN: 978-1-5064-8188-3

Contents

PREFACE   vii

1 LEARNING FROM SUBVERTED STORIES:
THE WISDOM OF NINETEENTH-CENTURY
BLACK WOMEN PREACHERS   1

2 ZILPHA ELAW: FOLLOWING THE SPIRIT'S
FOOLISH CALL   17

3 JULIA FOOTE: BODYING THE WORD   69

4 SOJOURNER TRUTH: THE SPIRIT'S WITHNESS   111

5 BLACK WOMEN PREACHERS AS EXEMPLARS
OF A PROPHETIC PASTORAL THEOLOGY   149

ACKNOWLEDGMENTS   167

NOTES   171

SELECTED BIBLIOGRAPHY   183

INDEX OF NAMES AND SUBJECTS   191

INDEX OF BIBLE PASSAGES   195

Preface

Every pastor-theologian has a story and a calling that precedes their sermons, writings, and ministries. In the coming pages, we will explore these called moments in the lives of nineteenth-century Black women preachers Zilpha Elaw, Julia Foote, and Sojourner Truth. Knowing their contexts helps us engage their theologies on a more profound level. Because I detail the importance of knowing their backgrounds, and really all theologians' backgrounds, when engaging their works, I feel it is only fair to offer my own background.

I write as a white middle-class woman, born and raised in a white moderate Baptist church tradition in Jefferson City, Missouri, the capitol of Missouri. I loved—and still love—my home church. My youth pastor was a young woman, my senior pastor supported my call to ministry, and caring adults surrounded me. In my teenage years, our downtown church began to identify itself with the Cooperative Baptist Fellowship, a breakaway denomination[1] from the Southern Baptist Church, because we supported women in ministry. The local Southern Baptist association finally kicked my home church out when we ordained a woman as an associate pastor.

I was not aware of my own white privilege growing up, though I could sense something awry within my community. Jefferson City had a historically Black university, Lincoln University, which Black veterans founded after the Civil War. Lincoln also functioned as a commuter school, educating both white and Black local residents. Both my dad and my uncle graduated from there. My neighborhood elementary school served some historically Black neighborhoods as well. Growing up, I developed relationships with Black students at birthday parties, through sports leagues, and in classroom settings. I learned from a few Black teachers, and we had projects related to Black figures during Black history month. Nevertheless, I more or less adopted a color-blind mentality, attempting a neutrality that I realize now was never neutral. This neutral racism was more of the polite variety—I did not hear slurs, but I would at times hear adults negatively speak about my elementary school. Local governmental agencies did not highlight or support Black organizations. There were economic disparities between where my Black and white classmates lived. The people who held power—local elected leaders, government heads, business owners—were all white. But I did not recognize the prejudice within myself, nor did I question or challenge racist stereotypes of the people around me. I simply stayed quiet.

In private Christian college in suburban St. Louis, I acutely witnessed the white supremacy that plagued evangelical Christianity. Students who studied ministry disparaged student athletes, many of whom were Black, Indigenous, and people of color (BIPOC), because from the ministry students' perspective, the athletes didn't seem interested in the required chapel services or the faith component of the school. Because athletes attended college for the scholarship opportunities and not necessarily the Christian atmosphere, they were deemed less holy than people who attended because of its Christian orientation. It seemed as if these mostly white ministry students thought that to be an athlete and a Christian, or to be a BIPOC and a Christian, was incompatible. I was both a ministry major and a not-very-good athlete and witnessed how my Black teammates had little support from either the coaches or the school administration as they navigated their college experience. Many transferred or left after one or two years. In academics, my Christian theology and ministry classes were solely taught by white men, and we solely read white authors. I felt unease about what I witnessed but was not sure how to respond, so I mostly ignored it.

Only in seminary and graduate studies did I begin to read BIPOC theologians. I entered my graduate studies with a general focus on examining humility through a theological lens. Not long into my coursework, I realized I could not speak honestly about humility without attending to the ways in which Black women have been humiliated, as Dr. Linda Thomas taught me in her Black and womanist theology class at Luther School of Theology–Chicago. The following year, in an African American religious history class, Dr. Larry Murphy lent me his copy of Margaret Washington's *Sojourner Truth's America*. While Washington is a historian, the way she theologized on Truth's sermons and autobiographies inspired me. For example, Washington called Truth an "African Dutch mystic," brought a confessional perspective to the story of Sojourner Truth, and articulated the origins of her theology by using Truth's background and upbringing to undergird her claims.

In that same class, I began reading William Andrews's *Sisters of the Spirit*, which provides the autobiographies of nineteenth-century Black women preachers Jarena Lee, Zilpha Elaw, and Julia Foote. I was amazed by the way these women theologized and by how their theologies led them to persevere in immense challenges. Andrews connects the dots biblically with their narratives; when they allude to Scriptures, he provided footnotes with biblical references. This allowed me to see how the women saw themselves as prophets and evangelists.

I wish I had encountered Black women preachers in my undergraduate studies, for they made a case for both Black women's preaching and the abolition of slavery and capital punishment in ways that depicted their commitment to God and love for their neighbors and for themselves. They took the Bible seriously, yet departed from those who advocated for biblical authority in enslaving people and prohibiting women in ministry. I realized that if I were to write anything about humility that held any weight and could be faithful to the liberating God I claim to follow, I had to include their witness. I could not talk about humility without talking about the humiliation Black women experienced in the United States and how white women had participated in and sanctioned such humiliation. I, as a white woman, had to own my own legacy of sin in dehumanizing Black women and the way this legacy still continues in my present actions. From my discussion on humility, I wanted Black women's narratives, sermons, and memoirs to be the primary theological texts I engaged. I read the women's words and witnesses and see them not only as preachers but as theologians who interpret Scripture, their own experiences, and the promptings of the Holy Spirit. Their stories convicted me of how my silence and passivity as a white woman were dangerous and sinful. By remaining silent, I sinned against my Black classmates and quenched the Spirit within me.

Encountering womanist theologian Joy Bostic's text *African American Female Mysticism: Nineteenth-Century Religious Activism* provided an exemplar for theologizing the narratives of nineteenth-century Black women. She read their autobiographies and sermons closely, honoring their contexts and stories while drawing out significant theological themes and conclusions. Bostic's creative theologizing illuminates my own. Discovering Professor Kimberly Blockett's research on Zilpha Elaw, including how Elaw modified her rhetoric based on her audience, opened my eyes to how Elaw's prophetic announcements came in ingenious rhetorical gestures and showed me her brilliance more deeply.

As a white woman writing about Black women, I realize the danger of misappropriation looms large. White women have had a history of dehumanizing Black women. At one of the earliest women's rights conventions, the Seneca Falls convention in New York in 1848, Elizabeth Cady Stanton and other women's rights leaders prioritized white women's rights and privileges while neglecting Black women. The racism exhibited there was, in part, why Sojourner Truth preached her sermon "Arn't I a Woman"[2] in 1853.

I follow the lead of Karen Teel, a white theologian writing about womanist theology. In her study of twentieth- and twenty-first-century womanist theologians, she asserts, "I study Womanist theologies because their values are human values."[3] Further, Teel writes that she studies womanist theologians not because they "cannot speak for themselves" but because "as a member of the oppressor group, I need to listen to Black women in order to recognize the part I have played in their suffering, to repent that role, and to be transformed."[4] Like Teel, I engage nineteenth-century Black women's narratives from my own perspective as a white Protestant American feminist theologian and pastor, learning from them how to love others and the divine more fully. I read and write about Elaw, Foote, and Truth because their stories matter. They inspire me, they convict me, and they encourage me when I despair. They present theologies that are deeply biblical and emphasize social justice, resisting twenty-first-century binaries we cannot seem to shake. More white people like me need to hear their stories, take seriously their words, and be amazed by their visions.

I now serve a United Methodist congregation in suburban St. Louis. I am still learning how to resist white supremacy and am continuing to become aware of where and how

I can do better. I learn how to be antiracist while recognizing that the church I serve was founded by an enslaver two hundred years ago. I believe the witness of Elaw, Truth, and Foote can help. In the church, I incorporate their stories in my sermons, devotionals, and teaching. I believe learning their theologies can help us follow the loving God we proclaim. I pray that this book is faithful to them as well, and dedicate this text to their withness.

1

Learning from Subverted Stories

The Wisdom of Nineteenth-Century Black Women Preachers

The nineteenth-century Black itinerant preacher Zilpha Elaw, upon hearing her only sister, Hannah, was ill, traveled to Philadelphia with her young daughter in tow to help care for her. Upon Elaw's arrival in her room, Hannah exclaimed, "My dear sister, I am going to hell." Elaw sat stunned, as a wave of visitors shuffled in and out of her sister's room. A few ministers told the Elaw to not be afraid. While the caregivers attended to Hannah, Elaw herself seemed to be merely witnessing the action, not involved as an active participant. As a group prayed over her, Hannah shouted, "Glory to God in the highest, and on the earth peace; for I again have found Jesus.'" Hannah then turned to Elaw, looked her in the eye, and exclaimed "Ah, Zilpha!

angels gave it me to sing, and I was told that you must be a preacher!"[1] After Hannah's death, Elaw wondered how *she* could be called to preach—she had no formal training or education, and as a Black woman, she knew the odds were stacked against her. Nonetheless, Hannah's words accompanied Elaw as she followed her sister's wishes in becoming a preacher, eventually traveling in England to proclaim the good news of Jesus.

Long before Julia Foote was the first woman deacon and second woman elder in the African Methodist Episcopal Zion Church, she found herself recently married and relatively isolated while her husband worked for long stretches on a cargo ship. To combat the loneliness, she immersed herself in church life, visiting the sick, attending Bible studies, and praying constantly. In that period, Foote sensed Christ's love overwhelming her soul, so much so that she had to share it with others. Yet she resisted God's calling "to a definite work," shrinking before the enormity of the task. Her heart became heavy, her appetite ceased, and her husband called the doctor to care for her. While praying, Foote received a vision where an angel told her, "Thee have I chosen to preach my Gospel without delay."[2] Foote was frightened and confused, for she "had always been opposed to the preaching of women and had spoken against it." She doubted this calling, asking God to make it plain, to prove it. Two months later, an angel visited her again, not unlike the story of Jonah: "You have I chosen to go in my name and warn the people of their sins," the angel said. She writes, "I bowed my head and said, 'I will go, Lord.'"[3] At that moment, Foote felt a wave of peace wash over her.

Born an enslaved woman in upstate New York, Isabella walked away from her enslaver and traveled to New York City to begin a new chapter in her life as a freedwoman. However, when she looked back on her time in the city, she felt disappointed in what she had to show for it. The utopian community she joined crumbled, and she realized its values were not aligned with what her Christian faith had taught, that she had to leave, to travel east, and to share the gospel elsewhere. She told the woman with whom she was boarding that "her name was no longer Isabella, but SOJOURNER." When asked why she was leaving, Sojourner responded, "The Spirit calls me there, and I must go." Well past the age of forty, she took only what she could carry and left. Like the disciples sent by Jesus, Sojourner Truth relied on the hospitality of others as she testified "of the hope that was in her" as she preached across the eastern and midwestern United States, encountering the likes of President Abraham Lincoln, Frederick Douglass, and Elizabeth Cady Stanton.[4]

The call stories of these three nineteenth-century Black women do not just mark the beginning of a formal, or at least documented, narrative history. Their subsequent accounts aren't just stories of survival and perseverance. They are creative works of theology situated in their particular communities. God calls them not only to preach but to theologize, and the witness they leave behind are works of theology that resonate with twenty-first-century concerns. Their theologies honored bodiliness, practiced relational empathy, and are mystically contemplative.

The nineteenth-century United States saw Black women's bodies as inferior in every aspect. The world around them consistently degraded their bodies. Sojourner Truth's enslavers valued her in the work she produced and the children she bore. A white man did not consider Julia Foote a lady as he burst into the ladies' cabin on a ship. Zilpha Elaw was paraded before the white antislavery society in England without them even asking her if she had ever been enslaved. While all three women, in their work, may occasionally have described themselves as weak or small, the entirety of their lives presented a different picture. They traveled miles across tough terrain, in rain and snow, in order to preach the gospel. As they received sanctification, they saw their bodies as conduits of the divine. They "gloried in their color," seeing their Blackness as a gift.[5]

Truth, Foote, and Elaw's appreciation for their Blackness came from the root understanding that they were created in the image of God. They sought the image of God—to establish a relational connection—in the people to whom they ministered, who came from all walks of life. Zilpha Elaw preached to high-ranking military officials and visited sex workers. Sojourner Truth met with President Abraham Lincoln and road the street cars with the working-class Black and white people. Julia Foote preached to hostile audiences, as well as in venues that were overflowing with people. The women followed the apostle Paul's urging to "become all things to all people."[6] Since they knew God loved their full selves, they sought to pass along that love to others in any way possible.

The women knew God loved their full selves because they had experienced God directly in mystical contemplation. For them, the divine was not only something to be studied or believed. God was an encounter too profound for words.

Sojourner Truth felt a bright light at the moment of her conversion, coming to a deepened understanding that God had always known and loved her. Zilpha Elaw saw multiple visions as she discerned her call to ministry. Julia Foote experienced a vision with allusions to the book of Revelation when she accepted her call to preach. The women had these mystical visions because they had spent time contemplating God and God's relationship with them. As they spent time in mystical contemplation, they realized God offered them a salvation that had material consequences in the present moment.

Because Truth, Elaw, and Foote understood salvation and wholeness as this-worldly as well as otherworldly, they indicted situations and persons who kept them and their communities from being whole. Their faithfulness to God meant that they contested whatever would deny their *imago Dei*–ness. The three women contended with white supremacy, sexism, and class struggles as they preached and taught. They could not address white supremacy without addressing sexism and class struggle. Their experiences of multiple forms of discrimination can be analyzed through the lens of intersectionality, which examines multiple factors in addressing oppression rather than focusing on a single issue like racism. As Kimberlé Crenshaw puts it, these women's theologies "facilitate the inclusion of marginalized groups for whom it can be said: 'When they enter, we all enter.'"[7] Elaw, Foote, and Truth's intention to present themselves as whole persons in all their particularities contested any single-issue analysis. Their theologies provided a way for everyone to enter.

The Method of Storied Witness:
Theologizing as a Just Endeavor

Historically, formal study of theology has focused on a top-down approach, whereby academics in schools train pastors who then educate people. In the United States, until relatively recently, most theological works studied in white seminaries and white churches were by white authors, which kept people's theological lenses narrow. This method of engagement also overlooked persons with less privilege who have produced theology in less traditional ways. In the United States, Black women have always been producing theology, even if not seen as legitimate by the academy. As Jocelyn Moody articulates, Black women "unquestionably produced theology. . . . Their life stories not only investigate black women's interior spiritual lives and the centrality of Christianity . . . but each woman also theorizes on who and how God is."[8] Around 1773, at age twenty, Phillis Wheatley theologized through her published book of poems. A native African enslaved and stolen to the United States, Wheatley wrote religious poetry as a teenager and young woman. Because she was enslaved and unable to express her views and theology freely, she wrote in a way that would appease and appeal to white audiences and their prejudices.[9] George Washington even wrote Wheatley to thank her for the poem she wrote about him.[10]

A number of Black women in the nineteenth century began to record their own theological journeys, like Jarena Lee, who published her memoir in 1836. Lee, born a freedwoman in New Jersey, began preaching after her pastor husband's death. She was the first official woman preacher in the African Methodist Episcopal denomination and the first Black woman to publish an autobiography in the United States.[11] As freed Black women continued to publish their insights, they were able to take a firmer stand against the white supremacy and misogyny that plagued their lives.

As outsiders to the established theological canon, nineteenth-century Black women preachers had the ability to speak truth and be prophetic in a way the white (theological, political, and economic) majority did not. They experienced firsthand the consequences of white majority theological commitments. Sojourner Truth refused to view the Bible as written by God and without error. She remembered how enslavers selectively took Bible verses about slavery and applied them to their nineteenth-century context with little reflection. Instead, her context led her to see that the people who penned the Scriptures "had intermingled with them ideas and suppositions of their own."[12] In challenging biblical infallibility, she could wrestle with Scripture on a deep level, allowing the Holy Spirit within her and the world around her to shape her biblical interpretation. Biblical interpretation was not for the sake of the spiritual realm only. Both enslavers and abolitionists used the Bible to justify their positions and influence laws. She noticed white people, who had not suffered the cruelties of slavery, interpreted the Bible as a weapon with proof texts rather than a book to wrestle with and learn from. Elaw and Foote would deploy this same logic Truth used with the Bible and apply it to other doctrines. If the consequence of a theological belief inhibited their freedom, they discarded or altered the belief.

Truth, Elaw, and Foote's witness also offers a way to reimagine how Christians view theological education. For a long time, people studying the subject read theological books without deeply considering the lived experience of writers. In addition, as people read theological texts, they did not consider how their own context shaped their viewpoints. The writers did not make their contextual realities specific as they laid out their ideas. Theologians from the margins were the first to interrogate how one's own context leads to theological conclusions, whether harmful or helpful. Elaw, Foote, and Truth implicated their circumstances as they referenced contemporary public documents or commented on enslavement by utilizing Scriptures. They did not have the luxury of ignoring the past or the present—and their role within the present—as they spoke about God. Like James Cone, who compared Jesus's crucifixion to white people lynching Black people in the United States, they saw dominant society as the Roman Empire and Jesus suffering alongside them.[13] The women did not present their theologies in a systematic way. Yet their conclusions aligned with theological loci, such as theological anthropology, Christology, and pneumatology. They each saw their theologies through to their practical implications. For example, the Spirit's indwelling of them in sanctification empowered them to affirm their humanity as beloved. Therefore, they could fight injustice that would deny their belovedness. To perceive theologizing as a just endeavor means taking seriously and centering the witness, stories, and thoughts of Truth, Elaw, and Foote.

Setting the Stage: Modes of Engagement

Theology and theologizing are never isolated endeavors, both in terms of community and in terms of discipline. Elaw, Foote, and Truth at times embraced solitude to discern and pray, but they always preached, theologized, and ministered in community. They used insights from their culture, along with biblical exegesis, to craft theologies that are simultaneously prophetic and pastoral.

Sociohistorical Context

While Elaw, Foote, and Truth, preached to different places, they lived in the cultural milieu of nineteenth-century United States and Great Britain. Knowing their general context illuminates their motivations and theological conclusions. The nineteenth-century United States experienced drastic changes: the rise of industrialization, the development of railroads, the Civil War, abolition and Reconstruction, and westward colonization (i.e., the pursuit of "manifest destiny").[14] In the midst of such changes, these Black preacher women remained faithful to their calling in a culture that often denied their humanity.

Cult of Domesticity

The cult of domesticity, or true womanhood, coincided with the Victorian era and stratified gender boundaries. To be a proper woman was to be white and middle or upper class and to not work outside the home. Such thinking revered piety and submission as the most important attributes for women.[15] The home, a private residence, was the women's sphere.

Zilpha Elaw, Sojourner Truth, and Julia Foote both abided by and subverted these ideals in order to legitimize their calls to preach. Black women automatically fell outside the Victorian ideals of womanhood due to their race, but at times, Elaw, Foote, and Truth made gestures toward its ideals. Sojourner Truth posed for a photograph in a nice dress with knitting needles, an image that complied with white women's cultural expectations of the day. In her memoir, Zilpha Elaw concurs that a wife is the helpmeet of her husband (from Genesis), provided he is a godly man, thereby acknowledging that she knew women's roles—even as, in the following paragraphs, she describes at length how her husband was not a godly man, and thus she could not submit completely to him.[16] Elaw also modified her rhetoric when addressing white audiences, knowing they would be appeased by more complicated sentence structure and vocabulary.[17] The introduction to Julia Foote's autobiography, written by "Thos. K. Doty," speaks of Julia Foote's disadvantages, which he calls "crimes," of "Color," of "Womanhood," and as an "Evangelist."[18]

These gestures toward white ideals of womanhood were perhaps a form of what W. E. B. Du Bois calls the "double consciousness." Elaw, Foote, and Truth had to know how to live and move in the culture of white America, even when it oppressed them.[19] Though they knew these Victorian ideals wouldn't let them live out their full callings, appeasing them at times was the way the women negotiated the world and sought power. Their appeals to white culture were strategic, if only so that white people might be more amenable to listening to them. In the Victorian era, their theologies that God gloried in their gender and their Blackness stood in stark contrast to the dominant narratives of the day.

US Political Landscape

In addition to navigating the role of women in the public sphere, Foote, Elaw, and Truth also had to negotiate living in the politically toxic climate of the pre–Civil War United States. Though the women were all from the North, the insidiousness of slavery shaped their upbringings, cultures, and outlooks. Racism was not just a Southern phenomenon, nor was enslavement. In fact, New York, where Truth grew up, had the largest population of enslaved people in the North.[20] Foote and Truth lived in the United States through the Civil War, while Zilpha Elaw was living in England by then. Foote does not chronicle the war in her memoir, but her writing demonstrates she knew of *Dred Scott v. Sandford*, which the Supreme Court decided on ten years before the war broke out, affirming the dehumanization of Black people as a policy. After the Civil War, racism loomed in the background as the women negotiated their roles as itinerant evangelists. Nonetheless, Elaw, Foote, and Truth affirmed and celebrated their humanity as Black women in a white world that saw them as lesser.

Truth, Elaw, and Foote's theologizing was shaped in large part by the Second Great Awakening. Historians characterize the Second Great Awakening as a Christian revivalist movement occurring in the first half of the nineteenth century. It emphasized conversion of the lost, emotional preaching, and congregational music. Key to the success of the Second Great Awakening was the camp meeting, an often weeklong revival service that drew people from various areas. Elaw, Foote, and Truth attended camp meetings, usually in rural areas. Julia Foote was present at a "bush meeting," which was a religious revival conducted in a grove of trees.[21]

The meetings drew thousands of people and created "temporary communities larger than most permanent ones in many regions." Zilpha Elaw saw "four or five thousand persons" in attendance, with a schedule of public prayers, worship, and fellowship. Elaw may have referenced that number in particular because that's the number of people Jesus fed in the Gospels.[22] She portrayed the camp meetings to her British audience this way: "Many thousands assemble in the open air, and beneath the overspreading bowers [shade from the trees] to own and worship our common Lord. . . . It is like heaven descended upon an earthly soil, when all unite to 'Praise God, from whom all blessings flow.' The hardest hearts are melted into tenderness; the driest eyes overflow with tears, and the loftiest spirits bow down, the Creator's works are gazed upon, and His near presence felt around."[23] Elaw could mystically contemplate God in community at the camp meetings.

These meetings also allowed for a lessening of social boundaries, though white supremacy was never eliminated. This tapering of limits related to class and race allowed Black women like Elaw, Truth, and Foote to preach and to witness the preaching of other women. For Elaw, the Methodist camp meeting was when she experienced sanctification: "It was at one of these meetings that God was pleased to separate my soul unto Himself, to sanctify me as a vessel designed for honor, made meet for the master's use."[24] Sojourner Truth saw camp meetings as an important part of her spiritual formation and beginnings as a preacher. Some of her primary ministry was at camp meetings. There, she preached, sang, and told people about their sins and about Jesus. Camp meetings, with their relaxed social boundaries and worshipful presence, provided a glimpse of God's kingdom. In Foote, Truth, and Elaw's understanding of the eschaton, Black women were celebrated for their preaching and theologizing, and people lived in peace under the Prince of Peace.

In part from the camp meetings, Elaw, Truth, and Foote learned about itinerant ministry. These preachers did not have one church to whom they were the called and settled pastor; rather, they went where the Spirit led them. They preached in both rural and urban areas, in both Black and white churches. While they may have found a home denomination, they often crossed denominational lines, preaching in Baptist, Methodist, and Quaker churches. Itinerancy enabled people at the margins to preach and minister. While itinerants generally preferred the blessing of a church, they did not need the sanction of the church hierarchy or denomination to preach the gospel. Elaw,

Foote, and Truth saw itinerancy as a creative way to theologize and preach even when not afforded traditional paths to ministry.

Elaw, Foote, and Truth were not commissioned by a denominational body at first. As Jennifer McFarlane-Harris highlights, they traveled extensively, imagining themselves as the disciples of Jesus or like Paul in his ministry journeys.[25] Foote writes of a minister, Mr. Beman, who vehemently opposed her preaching, and implied that the churches who welcomed her would be excommunicated. When Foote wrote a letter in which she expressed her concerns to the denominational leaders, they ignored it because of her gender. She left Boston for Philadelphia, where she received a warmer welcome. Foote preached among the Quakers, Methodists, and Baptists. Zilpha Elaw, too, preached among an array of denominations. She preached in Baptist churches in Massachusetts. When she suffered a grave illness, which weakened her so greatly that she couldn't even lift her hand, a Quaker woman cared for her. While Elaw preached to a wide variety of denominations, she rooted her identity in the Methodist tradition, and when she journeyed to England, she preached mostly among Methodist churches. Sojourner Truth, as an itinerant, preached among Baptists, Quakers, Methodists, and more, in addition to her abolitionist and suffragist lectures. Her faith in God compelled her not only to preach but to advocate for political and social concerns that would better her community. The ability to be itinerant, along with the presence of camp meetings and their relaxed social and denominational boundaries, alluded to the apostle Paul's letter to the Galatians: "All of you are one in Christ Jesus."[26] Truth, Elaw, and Foote embraced that saying fully, understanding themselves as being on equal footing with everyone they met and, simultaneously, seeking unity among the people they served. Being one in Christ Jesus served as an orienting metaphor for their theological tasks.

Storied Witness: Looking Ahead

Ultimately, Elaw, Foote, and Truth interpret Scripture and characterize a God who *favored* them and *loved* them, and their bodies, even when the world said otherwise. They were in awe of God's calling *them* and claimed that call to boldly share creative theology, even as they faced resistance. They developed mystical contemplative practices and celebrated their bodies as good and beloved.[27] Their theologies told their world the truth about God, justice, and judgment. Their theologies still tell the truth today.

2

Zilpha Elaw

Following the Spirit's Foolish Call

According to the mores of her world and of today, Zilpha Elaw is a fool. Generally, a fool lacks common sense and acts outside what is considered "normal behavior." A fool is often seen as harmless and silly, with no discretion as to what is "proper," and rendered to the margins of society.[1] As a Black American woman who claimed her calling as an evangelist in the nineteenth century, dominant (white) society in both the United States and England saw Elaw as foolish. She senses her foolishness—her marginality is one reason why God calls her. God works especially through her because of her weakness—her foolishness. The notion of weakness becoming a strength dominates Christian Scriptures, from the Hebrew prophets' hesitancy to accept their callings to Paul's declaration that power is made perfect in weakness. While the "paradox of God," or power being made perfect in weakness, is present in the discourse of all the women in this book, Elaw's foolishness enables her to craft a theology that honors her Black body as especially capable to speak truth and prophesy. Historian Kimberly Blockett describes Elaw's memoir as "a response to a preexisting body of journalism that had already constructed American Blackness as wretched servitude."[2] Elaw's presence counters such journalism and attitudes present in the mid-nineteenth century.[3] Her memoir presents a unique theology that exemplifies a power made perfect in weakness.

Only in December 2021 was a full annotated account of Elaw's *Memoirs of the Life, Religious Experience, Ministerial Travels, and Labours of Mrs. Elaw* published, edited by Blockett. Elaw wrote her *Memoirs* with a primarily white audience in mind; after all, "in the case of an antebellum Black woman preacher, most of the story could not be told if the book were to be sold."[4] Blockett's research provides the contextual realities behind the written words, and it details Elaw's life after she wrote her memoir. Despite the confines of race, gender, and class, Elaw's *Memoirs* presents a unique theology that celebrates her gifts and ability to discern and reveal the mystery of God in a way that would comfort, challenge, and convict her audience. This mystery, as the apostle Paul intones, is neither "in lofty words" nor with "a wisdom of this age" but is a foolish wisdom that defies expectations and confronts hard realities.[5] In 1 Corinthians 1:18, Paul connects foolishness with the power of God expressed in the cross. He continues on the theme of what he considers foolishness in verse 26: "Not many of you were wise by human standards, not many were powerful, not many were of noble birth." For Elaw, foolishness is both a choice and a category in which the dominant society places her. At times, Elaw defied common sense as she preached and traveled in hostile places. In other instances, her mere presence as a Black woman in dominant white society automatically categorized her as foolish. Foolishness lies outside hegemonic common sense, in which ideas become reality, or a way of life, without an interrogation of why or how. Hegemonic logic means not being able "to think outside . . . [the] box." Both the "ruling classes and civil society" accept the status quo as the true way of being.[6]

Elaw, like the apostle Paul, saw her foolishness as a gift that follows the way of the cross. The concept of God dying upon the cross seemed foolish to first-century Judeans. In the crucifixion, what seemed normal was exposed as false or harmful. In this foolishness of the cross, the values of the world were uncovered as corrupt, shallow, and insufficient. Elaw's preaching and presence modeled Jesus's foolishness—the fool who died upon the cross because he refused to give in to the values of the empire. In acting foolish, Elaw exposed the "civilized" powers as shallow and corrupt.

Elaw's life and memoir mimicked the foolishness Paul commends. An itinerant Methodist, she followed her calling to preach in both the United States and England despite the disapproval of many around her. She defied her husband's wishes in accepting her call to preach. She traveled from Virginia, a slave state, to Maine, where she was the only Black person around for miles. When she first arrived in England, she was met with indifference and disdain. In England, she chose to preach among Methodist congregations, even though some Methodist leaders themselves disapproved of women preaching. She wrote her memoir for her English audience. Her reliance upon the Holy Spirit sustained her in her foolishness. Her memoir subtly reveals a foolish theology that exposes the weaknesses of the dominant society and presents a liberating God who especially calls her as a Black woman.

Elaw's Early Life

Zilpha Elaw was born around 1790 in Pennsylvania, presumably in an urban area in a freed Black family.[7] She describes her parents as religious, instilling a love of God in her. Difficulties and sorrow pervaded her young life. Her mother gave birth to twenty-two children, but only three survived to adulthood. She died in childbirth when young Zilpha was twelve, and her father, stricken with grief, placed her younger sister Hannah with an aunt and young Zilpha with a white Quaker family, Pierson and Rebecca Mitchel, in an indentured servant type of arrangement. This was common for Black girls and teenagers in the freed North. Eighteen months later, her father died, leaving her an orphan. Elaw remained with the Mitchels until she was an adult but did not speak much of them, other than writing that they were "kind benefactors" in the wake of her parents' deaths.[8] Though they were Quaker, Elaw found a home in Methodist circles and would consistently align herself with Methodists throughout her life.

Elaw's Conversion: Mystical Foolishness

Like many spiritual biographies of her day, Elaw's conversion is first marked by sorrow over her own sin. In the aftermath of her father's death, she began to take her faith more seriously. She thought about her own sin, and how that might affect her relationship with God. For instance, while speaking with her friends, she caved into peer pressure and cursed. Immediately afterward, she "looked up, and imagined God looking down and frowning upon me: my tongue was instantly silenced."[9] Not long afterward, God beckoned her through a dream. At the time, she believed dreams were purposeful: "It was a prevailing notion in that part of the world . . . that whatever a person dreamed . . . was prophetically ominous, and would shortly come to pass."[10] She dreamed that the angel Gabriel proclaimed that "Jehovah was about to judge the world." Elaw, in horror, exclaimed, "Oh Lord, what shall I do? I am unprepared to meet thee." Awakened by the dream's terrors, she became quiet and fearful, arousing the suspicion of her mistress, Rebecca Pierson.[11] Rebecca tried to comfort her, saying it was only a dream, but fourteen-year-old Elaw was still shaken. Not long after this incident, she was able to attend Methodist meetings, which further convicted her of her sin. As she describes it, "The divine work on my soul was a very gradual one, and my way was prepared as the dawning of a morning." Her fear of judgment and conviction of her own sin prompted her to draw near to God.

A more positive experience prompted her conversion— that is, the moment she knew her sins were forgiven and she was safe in God's arms. She was milking the cow and singing a hymn found in many early camp meeting songbooks: "Oh, when shall I see Jesus, / And dwell with him above; / And drink from flowing fountains, / Of everlasting love. / When shall I be delivered / From this vain world of sin; / And, with my blessed Jesus, / Drink endless pleasures in?"[12] The hymn represents a longing for union with Jesus and a desire to be freed of sin. Interestingly, Jarena Lee, another Black woman preacher from the same time period, included the same hymn in her own memoir.[13] While milking, something prompted her to look back, away from the cow. She saw a figure come toward her: "He had long hair, which parted in the front and came down on his shoulders; he wore a long white robe down to the feet; and as he stood with open arms and smiled upon me, he disappeared." At first, she thought she imagined this apparition, but when she turned back to the cow, she saw, amazed, that "the beast of the stall . . . bowed her knees and cowered down upon the ground."[14] Based on nineteenth-century artwork of the time, she assumed the figure was Jesus.

She understood what she had seen was a mystical experience beyond reason, and still included it in her memoir years later. She knew her English audience would doubt the truthfulness of her claim and goes at length to affirm it: "The thing was certain and beyond all doubt. I write as before God and Christ and declare . . . that every thing I have written in this little book, has been written with conscientious veracity and scrupulous adherence to truth."[15]

Her vision sparked a sense of spiritual and mystical ecstasy: she writes, "The joy in the Holy Ghost . . . was beyond comprehension," and "My soul transported with heavenly peace and joy in God."[16] This moment of Jesus coming to her, and her blissful feelings afterward, gave "meaning and clarity" to her identity.[17] Through this experience, she felt affirmed in her relationship with God and knew deep within her that no matter what, she had obtained the peace of God, which surpasses all understanding.[18] While the vision would surely seem foolish to those who encountered her story, Elaw's insistence on its truthfulness aligns with Paul's exhortation of the foolish shaming the wise.

After this vision, she joined the local Methodist assembly, describing the affair in formal terms: "In the year 1808, I united myself in the fellowship of the saints with the militant church of Jesus on earth; and I can never forget that memorable evening." She presented her testimony to the itinerant preacher currently serving her chosen congregation. He questioned her motives and affirmed that it was only God's will, and not her visions, which confirmed her conversion. The preacher then entered her name "in the class book of the [Methodist Episcopal] society." Elaw left that meeting in prayer and elation, as "the light of God's countenance continually shone upon [her]." After that meeting, when she encountered difficulties or felt sad, she turned to God, elaborating this heightened relationship in mystical terms: "An overflowing stream of love has filled my soul, even beyond my utmost capacity to contain. . . . I could not imagine it possible for any human being to feel such gusts of the love of God, and continue to exist in this world of sin."[19]

After a six-month waiting period of good attendance and evidence of conversion, Elaw was baptized. For her, baptism implied the equality of all persons before God. To describe her beliefs about baptism, Elaw invoked 1 Corinthians 12:13: "For in the one Spirit we were all baptized into one body—Jews or Greeks, slaves or free—and we were all made to drink of one Spirit." As the pastor announced the trinitarian formula in baptism ("I baptize thee into the name of the Father, Son, and Holy Ghost"), Elaw says, "[I] was so overwhelmed with the love of God, that self seemed annihilated: I was completely lost and absorbed in the divine fascinations."[20] This "annihilation" is reminiscent of medieval mysticism, where both men and women were so absorbed into union with Christ that they found themselves "annihilated" in God. By describing her conversion in mystical terms, Elaw places herself as especially called by God as a preacher to share the gospel, even if she appears lacking in common sense (foolish) to the rest of the world. Appearing foolish to the world aligns her with the apostle Paul in 1 Corinthians 1:20, in which he declares, "God made foolish the wisdom of this world."[21]

After her conversion, Elaw suffered ridicule from both her mistress Rebecca and others around her. Her peers mocked her for converting to Methodism. They perceived Methodists as uneducated, overzealous, and foolish. Methodists would stubbornly travel across the country, preaching "to the ends of the earth," whether they were welcome or not.[22] Before her conversion, Elaw had made "saucy replies" to her mistress when corrected. After her conversion, she sought "habitual communion with God" and responded to her mistress with "the meekness and gentleness of Jesus." Her mistress, in turn, accused her of "sullenness and mopishness." Her mistress's verbal abuse led

Elaw to ache for her deceased parents and turn to God as a source of comfort. Elaw turned to God in her loneliness and to her Methodist class for a sense of belonging.[23]

Elaw and Marriage: Who's the Fool?

Elaw worshipped with her Methodist community and stayed on as an indentured servant for the Mitchels until she married Joseph Elaw in 1810. While Elaw expounds on her conversion and relationship with God in ecstatic and blissful terms in her memoir, she viewed her marriage as a source of frustration and heartbreak. Her husband saw her foolishness as not having divine origin. Though she met him at church, it was not until after they married that she realized his opposition to her faith. Reflecting back on her marriage in her memoir, she described him as a "very respectable young man" yet not "a sincere and devoted disciple of Christ." Elaw felt she had been tricked, in a way, into marrying her husband. She remarked, "My dear husband had been a member of the [Methodist] society to which I belonged and had been disowned by them; but I could not regard him as a backslider from religion, for I am of the opinion that he had never tasted the pardoning love of God." The Methodist society had kicked him out for not abiding by their strict standards of faith and living. At first, he promised her that he would go back to the church and change his ways, but he never followed through on it. Eventually, he began to actively resist her church attendance.[24]

When addressing her marriage in her memoir, Elaw directly engages the Bible passages used to subordinate women, and, in particular, wives to their husbands. As she wrote her memoir, she had already been preaching to thousands of people across the United States and England. Yet she felt she had to address texts that diminished women's authority. A woman, according to Elaw's reading of the Bible, is under the authority of her father until she marries, at which point the authority transfers to her husband. She cites 1 Corinthians 11:9, which, in the translation Elaw uses, the King James Version, states, "Neither was the man created for the woman; but the woman for the man." Elaw explains this subordination as "the foundation of the family and social systems" and writes that to go against this "is a very immoral and guilty act."[25] Here, she appeases the more literalist readers of her audience and the people whom she encounters who want to dismiss her because of her gender. But she renders male authority of women a private matter, limited to the confines of a marriage where both spouses were equally faithful to God. Because Elaw was an orphan, and her spouse was unbelieving, she did not need to abide by the standards she sets out.

She also addresses how a woman should respond should she find herself in a marriage with an unbelieving husband. The unbelieving spouse and the Christian spouse have thought systems that are so radically different that no "utmost stretch of courtesy on both sides [will] ever reconcile the radical opposition of their principles." According to Elaw, in such marriages, each person thinks they could convince their spouse that their side is best, and all that causes is endless strife and heartache: "Thus both of them are miserably deceived, and miss of that happiness they so fallaciously had dreamt of."[26] Elaw's first love and allegiance were to God, and if this caused strife in her marriage, so be it.

After the church excommunicated her husband, Elaw began to preach without telling him. After about two months of preaching, someone teased him, saying, "Josh, your wife is a preacher." He told them no in the moment and later asked Elaw if it was true. She replied that it was. He mocked her, saying, "I'll come and hear you, if I come barefoot." This insulted Elaw, who saw the church, and her vocation, as a place of reverence and respect, following the call of God. Her husband so disagreed and disrespected her that he would make a fool of himself, defying cultural norms, to show how silly she was for preaching.

Eventually, Joseph hesitantly came to see her preach. Afterward, she notes, "I think that conviction of the sinfulness of his state strongly fastened to his conscience, for he became much troubled in mind." His teasing turned to fear. He worried she would be a "laughing-stock," claiming that, as she writes, "it appeared to him so strange . . . that I should become a public speaker; and he advised me to decline the work altogether." In this moment, he did not deny her call or giftedness but only said he felt embarrassed that she was preaching. After all, as the man of the house, *he* should be able to control her. Her membership in the church, and her preaching behind his back, demonstrated her priority was the church, not him. His excommunication had created a rift that he would refuse to mend. While saddened over his lack of support for God's call on her life, she had work to do, for God, she writes, "informed me that . . . I could not . . . descend down to the counsel of flesh and blood, but adhere faithfully to my commission."[27] In defending her defiance of her husband and her call to preach, she quotes Galatians 1:16 in her memoir, likening herself to the apostle Paul, who followed God's calling to preach among the gentiles instead of consulting with others. God's directive, against the cultural mores of her day, foolishly superseded her husband's concerns and opinions.

After witnessing her preaching and watching her call develop, her husband perceived her as strange for wanting to pursue her vocation and, knowing she would be mocked, begged her to stop. At times, distraught over her actions, he said to her, "My dear child, we are undone."[28] Nonetheless, she could not and did not stop preaching. She was married to an unbeliever, and so the subordination she had committed to before had no bearing on her marriage or her calling. In defying her husband, Elaw also defied the cult of domesticity, a values system in the nineteenth-century North Atlantic that emphasized deference, submissiveness, and purity.[29] In her defiance, Elaw exposed patriarchy as a weak and false power, unable to control her. Elaw disrupted not only her husband's but the dominant culture's ideals as she preached. Refusing to submit to her husband's wishes, her identity figured as unstable to both herself and others; there remained no group she could fit into. In this sense, she was a liminal figure, unable to conform to any category. She realized if she chose to be a public figure, against her husband's desires, she could live out her calling as an evangelist—rendering her unstable. By preaching, she both affirmed her liminality as uniquely called by God and asserted her power as a free Black woman, able to choose God's calling over human restrictions.

In the same section in which Elaw preaches submission, she implies that when conditions make this impossible, such as the loss of a father or discovering a husband is an unbeliever, these rules no longer apply. Further, Elaw seems to take her experience of marriage and apply it universally in that she does not chastise or correct women who preach, nor does she mention their marital status. Elaw explains at length that "in the ordinary course of Church arrangement and order, the Apostle Paul laid it down as a rule, that female should not speak in the church, nor be suffered to teach; but the Scriptures make it evident that this rule was not intended to limit the extraordinary directions of the Holy Ghost . . . nor to be rigidly observed in peculiar circumstances." Her belief in Pentecost's universal proclamation, which descended upon women and men, "[qualified] both for the conversion of [people] and spread of the Gospel."[30] From her comments on her marriage and the question of women preaching, Elaw seems to suggest that the guiding of the Holy Spirit, as evidenced in the Scriptures, supersedes the actual letter of the Scripture. In other words, one needs the Holy Spirit to interpret texts, and the freedom of the Spirit coalesces with the interpretation of texts.

Her flexible views on marriage related to calling applied to other people as well. Once, while Elaw was preaching, a woman felt called by God to join the church. Upon hearing that the woman was unmarried and living with the father of her five children, her application for membership was rejected. Elaw remarks, "The marriage customs and laws set forth by God in the Scriptures, are so widely opposite from those of civilized nations in modern times" that it is difficult to determine how to connect the two. Thankfully, Elaw notes, the woman legally married her partner, and after that, both joined the church. Elaw did not fault the woman for not being married legally, yet knew that woman must jump through the hoops to obtain membership.[31]

Despite Elaw's husband's disapproval of her ministry, she never stopped loving or caring for him. After their prolonged disagreement, Elaw's husband became ill, and she took on the role of sole provider and caregiver for her husband and daughter. This put great stress on her, as she had to earn an income, care for him, and tend to her young daughter. Right before he died, Joseph admitted to Elaw that he was wrong in opposing her ministry and asked for her forgiveness. In his last moments, he seemed to change: "His countenance assumed such calmness and sweetness, that the neighbours who visited him observed the change." Elaw implies that in these last moments, he experienced the saving power of God. He told Elaw that "he hoped that the Lord would ever sustain [her]." He died on January 27, 1823—for Elaw, "a day never to be forgotten." When her friends offered to pay for the funeral, she declined, wanting to pay for it herself, as "it was the last thing [she] could do for him."[32] Despite their differences of opinion, she still loved him.

A Foray into Teaching: Elaw Resists Her Calling

After she buried her husband, Elaw found herself in debt over the funeral and not sure of her next steps. She had arranged for herself and her daughter "a situation of servitude" as a live-in housekeeper and nanny for a white family.

However, Elaw's health prevented her from performing the backbreaking work. Instead, she opened a school for Black children, which the Quakers partially funded. She emphasized the importance of her as a Black woman teaching Black children, whom white people "refused to admit into their seminaries." In the nineteenth century, a "seminary" was a higher educational institution that sometimes, though not always, conferred collegiate degrees. These seminaries were often segregated by sex.[33] Writing of this, she directly addressed racism within the United States, saying, "The pride of a white skin is a bauble of great value with many in some parts of the United States, who readily sacrifice their intelligence to their prejudices, and possess more knowledge than wisdom." She wished "men would outgrow their nursery prejudices" and cites Acts 17:26, in which it says, "[God] hath made of one blood all nations of men for to dwell on all the face of the earth."[34]

Although she saw the importance of education, her soul still stirred to follow God's call to preach the gospel. She had sat aside her preaching and itinerant ministry while her husband was ill and remained in a holding pattern after he died. Her school was improving, but her heart was set on preaching, and she wondered if God still called her. Would she be able to have the money and preach? Could she ever get out of debt? Her worries "quenched the Spirit," and she sunk into a deep sadness, unable to preach. Her congregation wondered why she did not preach anymore, and her daughter asked her what was wrong.

It was the question from her daughter that enabled her to shake herself out of the darkness—she saw it as a "reproof . . . sent from God, who . . . had put it into the mind of a child to utter it." She prayed that God would open her heart and mind to preach again and that she would have the courage to travel and follow God's call, even with her worries. Three weeks before school was to end, some friends visited Elaw and encouraged her to preach, claiming, "He that sends thee will take care of thee." Elaw saw this visit as a confirmation of her ministry, and with tears in her eyes, she went home to pray. Her daughter again affirmed her calling, telling her, "Do not think any thing about me, for I shall do very well."

As she was teaching and asking the students to read the psalms, a student read Psalm 125:1, "They that trust in the Lord shall be as Mount Zion, which cannot be removed." Elaw saw this as further confirmation of her calling to preach, and after school ended, she had a relative care for her daughter and went to Philadelphia to continue her itinerant ministry.[35] While teaching might have felt like the safer occupation, the Spirit's calling Elaw could not be ignored, and she foolishly pursued it, against cultural norms.

In and Out of Season: Elaw's Foolish Preaching in the United States

Throughout her ministry, Zilpha Elaw, as a Black woman, was considered "foolish," according to the standards of hegemonic common sense, for her itinerant preaching. Her biblical exegesis highlighted such foolishness. When Elaw first began to live into her calling of ministry while her husband was still alive, her Methodist "class," like a small group or Sunday school class, began to turn against her, and eventually all but three of them abandoned her. They were jealous of her popularity. While the ministers affirmed her calling, the class still saw her as one of them, unqualified to hold any special authority. In her memoir, she likens herself to biblical characters: "Like Joseph I was hated for my dreams; and like Paul none stood with me."[36] By proclaiming her situation analogous to the character of Joseph in Genesis, she implicated that although the world considered her an outcast, her witness could bring salvation to others. Like Jesus in Luke 4, she was a prophet everywhere except within her own community.

Elaw's reference to Paul comes from 2 Timothy 4, which her contemporaries thought to be attributed to Paul, but today is thought to be a deutero-Pauline letter. In 2 Timothy 4:2, the author urges the community to preach the gospel "in season, out of season"—always and consistently.[37] This reflects Elaw's urgency and insistence as she encounters opposition. The author exhorts the church to do the ministry, even while they are suffering. Then in 2 Timothy 4:16, the author gives out final instructions to the community, explaining, "At my first answer no man stood with me, but all men forsook me: I pray God that it may not be laid to their charge."[38] Gathering from the context, Paul saw himself abandoned by his fellow believers when he was arrested the first time, but he forgave them, proclaiming that the Lord stood by him, and his arrest allowed him to share the gospel with the gentiles. By likening herself to Paul, Elaw established authority even as other ministers challenged or rejected that authority. On many occasions along her journey, she felt abandoned by religious authorities, yet she followed the call to preach the gospel in and out of season.

A Foolish Foray in the South

Elaw's foolish ministry continued as she discerned God's calling for her to preach in the southern United States, which at the time, upheld slavery. She likened herself to the biblical character Jonah, who reluctantly responded to God's sending him to preach to the large city of Nineveh.[39] As she traveled southward, "where slavery is established and enforced by law," a great fear seized her: "Satan suggested to me . . . that the slave-holders would speedily capture me." The novelty of a Black woman preacher in the South sparked curiosity among residents, drawing a big crowd to hear her preach. As she was preparing to take the pulpit in one of these Southern churches, she felt as if all fingers pointed toward her and was afraid. Minutes before the service was to start, she left the sanctuary to collect herself. She prayed for strength from God, exclaiming, "Get thee behind me Satan, for my Jesus hath made me free." This, of course, alludes to when Satan tempted Jesus for forty days in the wilderness in the Synoptic Gospels. After this moment in prayer, she resumed her position in the front of the sanctuary, ready to take her turn at the pulpit. She could preach with a peaceful mind, sensing the Lord's powerful presence within her. Her sermon inspired the white Methodists so much that they asked her to preach again that same afternoon to a larger audience. After receiving permission, authorities opened the county courthouse for her to preach, and she drew a large crowd.[40] Received positively by the crowds, she continued her journey in the South, explaining about herself, "The weakness and incompetency of a poor coloured female but the more displayed the excellency and of the power to be of God." It's impossible to know if she truly thought of herself as incompetent, based on her skilled vocabulary and the way that she criticized those in power. This could have been a rhetorical move to align people to her side or to show how ridiculous the current norms were.[41] Regardless of her intentions, she aligned herself with the foolishness of God, which shames the wisdom of the world.

Word spread of Elaw's work to the extent that enslavers around Alexandria, Virginia, became curious and invited Elaw to preach. In her sermon to these enslavers, she depicts them as thinking "it surpassingly strange that a person (and a female) belong[ing] to the same family stock with their . . . [enslaved people] should come into their territories and teach the enlightened proprietors the knowledge of God, and more strange . . . when in the spirit and power of Christ, that female drew the portraits of their characters, made manifest the secrets of their hearts, and told them all the things that ever they did."[42] Here, she declares solidarity with the enslaved people and insinuates she (and implicitly, they) express deeper spiritual insight than the enslavers. She identifies this as a paradox: though the enslavers had numerous ministers, seminaries, and financial support, they had nothing that compared to Elaw's wisdom. Again, referencing Paul's foolishness in 1 Corinthians 1:27, Elaw declares, "God hath chose the weak things of the world to confound the mighty."

Further, in her sermon to the enslavers, Elaw compares herself to Jesus in explaining that she "told them all the things they ever did." In the Gospel of John, Jesus tells the woman at the well in Samaria "all that ever [she] did."[43] Elaw purposefully connects the white Virginians—those living in the slave states—to the Samaritans of the New Testament, who, like the woman at the well, are associated with heresy and considered enemies of Jesus's community.[44] By purposefully seeing herself as (and acting as) a Christic figure, Elaw exemplifies "foolishness"—how could she, a Black female preacher, be considered like Christ vis-à-vis the white enslavers? This was outside the realm of the white enslavers' idea of common sense. She engages in a "social role reversal" as she claims spiritual authority.[45] She as Christ *is* sacred, not just a "vessel designated for honor," as she depicted herself elsewhere in her *Memoirs*, but especially holy precisely *because* of her Black female body.[46] In that moment, she was representing Christ to the enslavers.

Further, in telling the enslavers "all the things that ever they did," she questions their comfort with their own selves and in their own communities. While she does not list exactly "all the things" in her memoir, her sermon convicts the enslavers who listen to her. Alluding to the Johannine story, she equates the enslavers' position to that of the enemies of Jesus. Like the Samaritans in the Johannine text, the enslavers are not right with God, and Elaw sees it as her mission to highlight this reality. Fully knowing her vulnerability and precarity, she willingly preaches a sermon that exposes the sins of the enslavers, the most powerful group listening to her in the South.

Wherever Elaw journeyed in the South, people would ask her to preach. In Alexandria, Virginia, people would "flock" to the house where she stayed and beg her to preach after she had finished a meal with her hosts, "whether [she] had previously intended to preach or not." A Quaker friend, Abjiah Janney, commented on Elaw's ability to preach effectively to both white people and Black people—enslaved, enslaver, and freed. Elaw pondered her role, and her ability to communicate to a wide audience: "I was in connexion with two distinct communities, so opposite in condition . . . so antipodal in their feelings and prejudices."[47] While the gospel—the life, death, and resurrection—of Jesus Christ was the same, how she preached it and what people took from it were different things. White people of privilege heard judgment. Black people heard hope.

While Elaw planned the Scriptures she would preach upon in advance, she did not write them out in manuscript form. Instead, she knew the Holy Spirit was present within her and that reality guided her preaching method. Occasionally, she could not discern how God was directing her to preach. As Elaw was talking with a friend about her difficulty in selecting a passage to preach, 2 Kings 20:1 came upon her, but she couldn't figure out how to preach it. In this biblical passage, the prophet Isaiah is telling King Hezekiah that Hezekiah wouldn't recover from his illness, and he should prepare for his death. She paged through her Bible for an easier passage to preach, working until midnight Saturday and then waking before dawn on Sunday. When the time came, "as a criminal goes to the bar," she went to the grove where she would preach. Even for a prepared preacher, the act of giving a sermon can be nerve-wracking. Elaw, haunted by this passage and with no direction, felt an impending sense of dread. At the beginning of the service, she asked for an extra hymn to be sung. After the hymns, as she anxiously approached the pulpit, her "mind took a comprehensive grasp of the subject."[48] Suddenly, she was able to preach on the verse; she writes, "A region of truths were unfolded to my view, such as I had never previously conceived of." The Holy Spirit enabled her to preach more than ninety minutes on the subject. Like Elaw's conversion experience while milking the cow, this instance points to the mysticism inherent in Elaw's work and ministry—she had a "direct encounter with God" that freed her to preach truths she had never considered.

Elaw's journey in the southern United States included more difficulties. In Alexandria, she was invited by a well-to-do woman whose husband, a major in the military, had the habit of engaging in debates with the ministers she brought over. In Elaw's instance, he brought his friends, "who had been introduced for the purpose of testing my poor feminine abilities." Elaw engaged him with intelligence in a way that "he appeared highly gratified."[49] Elaw credits the Holy Spirit for her ability to match wits with this educated, high-ranking military major. He had intended to make her a fool, but Elaw, in the vein of Paul in 1 Corinthians, proved that the foolishness of God is wiser than human wisdom.[50]

When she traveled to nearby Washington, DC, she encountered people asking her to go to Africa to evangelize the people there. She remarks, "I declined their proposal; telling them, my heavenly Father had given me no such direction." At that time, major Protestant denominations in both the United States and England were forming mission boards and sending missionaries to Africa. White people thought that Black people would adapt to the African climate better and began sending Black American missionaries to Africa.[51] Because she was Black, Elaw's conversation partners assumed she would have the most success ministering among and to Black Africans. Perhaps sensing the racism in their assumption, she asserted that unless she received direction from God, she would not go there. This seemed to quell their curiosity for the time being.[52]

While in DC, a prominent group of women asked her to preach at a chapel used by missionaries. In her memoir, Elaw mentions the leading women by name: Lady Lee and Lady Rodgers, both of whose husbands were high-ranking officials in the military.[53] It seemed that Elaw's audience came not to hear the gospel but out of "motives of curiosity." People from "all grades of society" came to hear her. Elaw's sermon was so powerful that Lady Rodgers was converted: "The Lord was pleased to give efficacy to the word of His grace, and to apply it with saving power to the mind of Lady Rodgers." After Elaw preached the sermon, "a mighty religious awe and solemnity rested upon the entire assembly."[54] She left, grateful to God for moving among the people.

After sojourning with Southern elite families like the Rodgers and the Lees, Elaw traveled to Annapolis, Maryland, to spend the winter. On one occasion, after she finished a sermon there, an enslaved minister took the pulpit. She describes him as a "poor brother in bonds . . . very impatient of slavery, and anxiously sighed for liberty.

Alas! His life and spirit, his body, his bones, and his blood, as respects this life, were legally the property of, and at the disposal of his fellow man." Not even a week after Elaw witnessed his preaching, he became sick and died. Elaw remarks that it was only in death, falling "asleep in Jesus," that he could find release. Elaw quotes Job 3 that in death "the servant is free from his master." Attending the funeral, she acutely felt the grief of the congregation, whose cries interrupted the ministers officiating the service. Sensing the deep grief at the funeral, she lamented on the institution of slavery: "Oh, the abominations of slavery! Though Philemon be the proprietor, and Onesimus the slave, yet every case of slavery, however lenient its inflictions and mitigated its atrocities, indicates an oppressor, the oppressed, and the oppression. Slavery in every case . . . involves a wrong, the deepest in wickedness of any included within the range of the second table."[55] In the Pauline epistle of Philemon, Paul urges Philemon, the enslaver, to release Onesimus, the enslaved, after Onesimus becomes a Christian. While Elaw acknowledges that Onesimus's freedom was from Paul's command because Onesimus was a believer, she infers that the whole institution of slavery, even in the different context of the biblical period, always has involved an oppressor, the oppressed, and oppression—this cannot be escaped. Elaw remarks again toward the end of her journey in the "Slave States of America" how, as a freed Black woman, she feared for her life while ministering there.[56] The laws allowed white people to arrest and enslave any person of color "unless such person [could] produce the most unexceptionable papers in proof of his freedom." For all the time she was in the South, she was never asked once for the papers. She attributes that to God's providence: "[God] preserved me in my going out and coming in."[57]

Through Many Dangers: Elaw's Ministry in the North

Though Elaw feared enslavers might capture her in the South, as she entered the freed states, she encountered more concrete prejudice. While in New York, her mind "was disquieted," and she wasn't sure she should go to preach in a particular area. Her friends laughed it off. However, as she prepared to enter the building, a group of people blocked the entrance, and once the door was unlocked, this group came and sat up in the front to mock her. A large man came up to her, and as Elaw describes the incident, "[He was an] unusually stout and ferocious looking man: he came close up to me . . . as if he intended to seize or strike me." Though she knew something was off-kilter, she "felt no fear." He then sat by his friends and mocked her "in derision of the Methodists." She paused from her sermon and spoke to him personally, saying his soul was at stake, and he would be accountable to God. She then returned to her sermon with him in mind. The next day, he asked her to visit with him and pray with his family. She did and prayed that he might seek God's forgiveness. Fifteen minutes after she left, he died from a "rupture of a blood-vessel in the lungs." Word got out, and Elaw's visit to him "caused the fear of God to rest upon many."[58] Elaw's boldness in addressing him personally led him to become more open to her and perhaps convert to Jesus.

Danger also came in the form of discrimination when she tried to board a boat up North. At first, the captain refused, saying they had no room. Elaw suspected it was because she was Black. She found another boat that was leaving in the evening, where the captain agreed to take her. She thankfully boarded the boat and got settled.

Apparently, word had gotten around that Elaw was a preacher, and a man had asked her to preach for its passengers. Elaw at first was skeptical—she thought the passengers' intention in asking was pure curiosity at the idea of a Black woman preaching. Would they mock her? After one man obtained the captain's approval for it, she preached to about sixty people on board. Again, she sensed the men speaking about her and was anxious that they could be mocking her. But when they approached her, they thanked her for her sermon and expressed gratitude that she came on this ship instead of the earlier one. They gave her money for her ministry. Amazed at "the kind providence of [her] indulgent God," she realized the money covered her travel expenses, and then some.[59]

Elaw continued to preach despite resistance from those who would discount her ministry. While preaching in Hartford, Connecticut, the "principalities and powers of evil spirits (Ephes. vi. 12) . . . obstructed me much" and inspired powerful men "with a hostile zeal against me."[60] In particular, a Presbyterian minister named Mr. House "resolutely declared he would have my preaching stopped." Elaw likened House to the character of Sanballat in the book of Nehemiah in the Hebrew Bible: "Mr. House, resolutely declared that he would have my preaching stopped; but he, like Sanballat, imagined a vain thing." Sanballat, an official of King Artaxerxes while the Jews were in exile, mocked Nehemiah and the Jewish people, saying that they would never rebuild the walls of Jerusalem.[61] Sanballat also attempted to throw Nehemiah offtrack and distract him from the task at hand. Her English readers and her contemporary audience may have known who Sanballat was, and if not, she had proved she knew the Scriptures better than they.

Elaw had more important things to attend to than arguing with her detractors: "While the opponents of my ministry were pursuing their plans of opposition, it happened that I was sent for one day to visit a Mr. Freeman, who was dangerously ill." Apparently, Mr. Freeman had some clout, because the physician who visited him while Elaw was praying with him was "in the highest rank in society" (presumably white). The physician waited until Elaw finished praying with Mr. Freeman to enter. When the physician attended to Mr. Freeman, he was surprised to find him "much better," exclaiming, "It is the woman who has made you better." Elaw quickly remarked that she did nothing, but it "was the power of God through faith in the name of Jesus." The physician wanted to hear her preach, as he had heard that "[her] ministry had been attended by persons of every rank in life."[62] The physician even spoke to his minister, Rev. Mr. House, "the very gentleman who had declared that he would stop [her] from preaching in that city," about Elaw's calling and preaching. Rev. House responded, "Well, if God has sent her, I bid her God's speed." Elaw continued preaching throughout the city. She implies that she visited brothels, calling them "houses of ill fame." Her preaching was effective, as "many of these unfortunate females became genuine disciples of Jesus."[63]

Foolish Yearnings: Elaw's Desire to Preach in England

Throughout her travels in the United States, Elaw often felt called to preach in England, even when people questioned her reasoning for traveling across the Atlantic. England was a Christian nation; many she encountered didn't think it needed missionaries. Nonetheless, she saw signs pointing to her effective ministry and wondered if it was confirmation of her calling. While discerning whether to go to England, she witnessed the same vision three times. Her vision corresponded to the apostle Paul being caught up in the third heaven in 2 Corinthians 12. (While Elaw doesn't make the number "three" explicitly connected to the apostle Paul, one can intuit that experiencing the vision three times corresponds to Paul's third heaven.) Further, like Paul, she experiences being in her body yet also in a mystical place.[64] In 2 Corinthians 12, the apostle Paul "was caught up into Paradise and heard things that are not to be told."[65] In Elaw's vision, she was "caught up in spirit, away from and far above all sublunary things." Thousands of people surrounded her, all clothed in white, including herself. She explains, "I was employed in addressing this immense concourse."[66] In that vision, Elaw does not declare the message she was preaching, but by aligning herself with Paul, she establishes herself as an authority to her mostly white English readers.[67]

As she was still deciding whether to go to England, she met a bishop who asked what she would do if people thought that she was only preaching to attract attention and stir up trouble because she was a woman. She responded that her calling was from God to preach the gospel, and "therefore, [she] had no option in the matter." Thus, she portrayed people who were bothered by her ministry as "ignorant and prejudiced . . . men whose whims are law, who walk after the imagination of their own hearts, and to whom the cause of God is a toy." She could not and would not give in to their objections and neglect God's calling for her ministry. Her calling to itinerant ministry was so distinct that she remarks, "It is an easy matter to adopt a string of notions on religion and make a great ado about them; but the weight of religious obligation, and the principle of conscientious obedience to God are quite another matter."[68] Elaw implies that it is easier to become legalistic over doctrine than to obey God's calling on our lives. Those who are legalistic may look at those following God as foolish.

She felt called to go to England in her devotional time, though she tried to reject it by, in her words, "pleading my ignorance, my sex, my colour and my inability to minister the gospel in a country so polished and enlightened, so furnished with Bibles, so blessed with ministers, so studded with temples." Nevertheless, she felt the Lord insisting. She read Jeremiah 1:7, where Jeremiah claims ignorance, and God tells him that God will provide for him. Then she describes another vision where she was "placed upon an animal, which darted with [her] through the regions of the air, with the velocity of lightning." Through this vision, God told her clearly, "I have a message for [Elaw] to go with upon the high seas, and she will go."[69]

Elaw received confirmation from several people—rich and poor, Black, and white—on her last itinerant journey in the United States: "Without any solicitation of mine, they presented me their cheerful contributions; yea, both white and [Black] brethren, voluntarily came forward with their free-will offerings, to enable me to undertake the voyage, and bade me go and preach to strangers in a strange land." The phrase "stranger in a strange land" comes from the Bible. In Exodus 2:22, when Zipporah, Moses's wife, gave birth to their firstborn son, Moses named him Gershom because, he said, "I have been a stranger in a strange land." Here, Elaw likens herself to Moses, who delivered the Hebrews from slavery. By comparing herself to Moses, Elaw sets the stage for her ministry in England. Her goal would be to provide spiritual liberation for the English people, as a "stranger in a strange land."

Elaw glimpsed a foretaste of interactions with the English people when she attended the anniversary of the "abolition society" (known as the American Anti-Slavery Society) in New York before journeying to her daughter to prepare for her departure. The abolition society was cofounded by William Lloyd Garrison, and its members included prominent Americans, like Frederick Douglass and Lucretia Mott, along with ministers and activists and journalists.[70] Many of those speakers at the anniversary celebration had been at the original antislavery gathering at Exeter Hall in London.[71] Interestingly, Elaw would later encounter abolitionists in England, who gave her a cool reception.

She stayed with her daughter while getting ready to leave for London. Like Jeremiah or Isaiah, who trembled at the thought of God using them, Elaw felt a sense of holy fear. On her departure date, June 10, 1840, she arose early, noting, "The morning was calm, our minds resigned and peaceful, and we took, and held each other's hand in silence."[72] She knew that there was the possibility that she wouldn't be able to visit her family again and wanted to hold them as long as she could. Eventually, her daughter spoke: "Mother, we part now, but I think we shall yet meet again; the will of the Lord be done." At 9:00 a.m., she left her family and traveled to New York, where she boarded a ship to London. She wanted her English readers to know her grief over leaving her family and the conflictedness with which she followed God's call. "The parting moment was painful in the extreme," and years later, in this retelling, tears swelled in her eyes, and the memories made it so she could barely write. Nonetheless, she saw herself as Abraham, citing Genesis 12:1, whom God commanded to leave his home and his family and go to a land that God would show him. Her grief "was acutely indescribable," she writes, "but God commanded, and I obeyed . . . committing my dear friends to the grace of God."[73]

While she had traveled by ship before in the United States—and indeed, had traveled extensively across the United States—she had never journeyed across the ocean. Amazed at the expanse of sky and sea, she "surveyed the broad canopy above, and the rolling ocean beneath, gently moving wave after wave." She writes, "[I] observed the birds of the air flying over our heads and wondered, at such a distance from land, that they were able to take such excursions without resting."[74] In that wonder, she cites Psalm 104, which highlights specifically God's creation of the sea and its creatures. She and the fish, birds, and creeping creatures of the ocean all depended on God's provision.

Elaw's England Adventures

On July 26, Elaw stepped off the boat and onto the London Docks. As soon as Elaw stepped ashore, culture shock hit her. She departed from the ship on Sunday and was immediately surprised by the number of businesses open on "the Lord's Day." England, which supposedly was the most Christian country in the world, the country that people were confused as to why she was going, seemed to disregard the fourth commandment's order to observe the Sabbath. She remarks, "If Christians are not bound to observe an absolute quietude and rest thereon, they certainly are bound to pay it that respect which is due to the day on which or redemption was assured by the Lord's resurrection." She realized that England was not as Christian as people had told her and needed an evangelist like her to share the gospel.

Elaw struggled much more with her ministry in England than she had in the United States. The British were not as receptive to the gospel she preached, and she wrestled to understand why. At this point, the Second Great Awakening was winding down in both the United States and England. She wondered if the lower population density in the US, along with a less active printed press, made for "less . . . contamination" by sin there than in England.

This first impression of England, along with others, left her despondent. She would go days without meeting any other Methodists. Though John Wesley, one of the founders of Methodism, hailed from England, she struggled to find Methodist communities. Methodism had been where she was converted and nurtured and where she had had most success preaching, so the absence of a Methodist gathering left her feeling isolated and without a home.

Eventually, she found a Methodist community and met people who helped her make connections. One day, she encountered a woman "whose appearance powerfully arrested my attention; and it appeared that the feeling of surprise and interest was mutual." Elaw asked the woman if she knew of any Methodist societies that were meeting nearby. The woman introduced Elaw to her daughter, who in turn brought her to a Wesleyan chapel where several class meetings were held. With these classes, Elaw "enjoyed a very sweet time of refreshing from the presence of the Lord." She had found her spiritual companions in the Methodist society. One man she met had numerous connections and "interested himself greatly on [her] behalf." He had connections beyond Methodist circles. Awkwardly, and probably because of her race, he quickly "ushered [her] before the committees of the peace and anti-slavery society." This was not long after she had attended the anti-slavery society in the United States. It was also not long after the World Anti-Slavery Convention in London.[75]

In her memoir, she expresses her annoyance at being put on display before the white antislavery society. She mocks how they take themselves so seriously: "It was really an august assembly; their dignity appeared so redundant, that they scarcely knew what to do with it all." The anti-slavery society asked her question after question, such that

Elaw remarks, "I think I could scarcely have been more closely interrogated or more rigidly examined."

The antislavery society assumed she wanted money from them, thus their intense questioning. She could feel the power they attempted to hold over her and held her own in response to their questions. They asked her what she, a Black American woman, could offer to a Christianized England. She responded by quoting 1 Corinthians 1:23, where Paul claims to preach "Christ crucified," which is "foolishness" to the gentiles. They inquired who sent her, and she responded that God did, and she was obeying God, who knows best. They asked her how she knew God sent her, whether she had a new teaching, and what proof she had of her calling. She responded in the language of the calling of the prophets: "The Almighty's design therein was best known to Himself; but behold, said I, 'I am here.'"[76]

She then makes an aside: "Pride and arrogancy are among the master sins of rational beings," implying her interrogators expressed haughtiness in their questioning. On the other hand, she describes herself like Jesus, "meek and lowly," bearing witness "against the lofty looks of man, and the assumptions of such lordly authority." Elaw's resistance to being stereotyped as an enslaved person by the antislavery society emphasized her full self as a complex prophet. She believed her oddity as a Black woman preaching allowed people to listen to her, even in the supposedly Christian nation of England. England was full of churches and preachers, but people "had scarcely heard a sermon in their lives" and were "attracted to hear a [Black] female preacher." Because she incarnated Christ in her Black body, she ministered to them in a way white preachers could not. She revealed their blind spots to them.[77] Her words cut through the abolitionists' motives, revealing their desires for adulation. While they assumed she wanted some form of help, through her preaching, she brought the gospel to them in a way they had not been able to understand before, actually helping them.

News of Elaw's ministry grew, and she began to travel throughout England with various levels of success. She traveled to wherever she was invited, preaching first in the London area, then expanding to other cities. For the most part, during her time in England, she stayed with congregants or ministers as part of her ministry. Liverpool, unfortunately, was replete with discouragement. She thought she had secured lodging, but upon arrival at the designated location, found her female hosts absent and that her male host did not know of the arrangement. She was unable to stay with them. After this experience, she comments that this family had gone against the biblical admonishment in Hebrews 13, which tells its audience to not neglect to show hospitality to strangers. Instead, she used what little money she had to find a place to stay. Finally, she found some Wesleyan Methodist leaders, named in her memoir as Mr. and Mrs. D., who provided lodging. Mrs. D. began talking with Elaw and soon began berating her for wanting to preach, as it was against the Scriptures.[78] Elaw responded she could not "possibly understand" how her ministry, which brought people to Christ, could be construed as having authority "over the male sex." Mrs. D. then suggested Elaw join the Quakers, who allowed women's preaching. Elaw responded that God sent her to minister among the Methodists. After Elaw shared her certifications of ministry (letters from other ministers testifying the validity of her call), Mr. D. joined the criticism, claiming Wesleyan Methodists "do not allow women to preach." Elaw judges his tone had the indication "in which the commission of the Almighty is assumed." He seemed to have seen himself as empowered by God to judge such matters. Upon reflection, she remarked, "For the line of worldly wisdom . . . can never gauge the operations of the Spirit of God; and always either rejects them at once, or meets them with 'How can these things be?'" This reflects not only the "foolishness" of God but Elaw's strong pneumatology. Worldly wisdom would suggest that it was improper for Elaw to preach, but Elaw, filled with the Holy Spirit, knew the foolishness of God—that power made perfect in weakness—could not match up with such "worldly wisdom." Not deterred, she wondered privately if perhaps *he* should be examined for fitness for ministry, based on his rude behavior. Sensing her unwanted presence, she departed, declaring their house an "iron-hearted abode."[79]

That was not the only time Elaw encountered sexism in England. Elaw describes a time after she had preached at the Wesleyan chapel in Newbottle. The Newbottle congregation was so impressed with her preaching that they invited her to preach again at a later date and also invited her to a tea meeting a week later. In British Wesleyan churches, tea meetings were social gatherings where members could meet for fellowship and discuss the business of the church.[80] While she did not receive any confirmation about a specific time she should preach, she did receive a ticket to the tea meeting. But when she arrived and presented her ticket, they would not allow her in: "They had all forgotten me; nor was there one who was able to recognize the preacher who had so delighted them the previous week." Elaw thought that someone had probably told them the dangers of women's preaching: "They had probably received a philippic from some petty Authority against female preachers, which had blotted me out altogether from their thought and feeling."[81] Identifying the authority "petty" legitimizes her calling. Even though she's seen as foolish—outside of societal common sense—by the Newbottle chapel, it's the petty authority who's actually foolish, failing to recognize the indwelling Holy Spirit within Elaw.

In Manchester, she had more luck with her ministry. A woman had gone to see Elaw preach the week prior, and while Elaw's sermon had greatly affected the woman, she still suffered a disheartened countenance. As Elaw visited her in her bedroom, she took the woman's Bible and opened it up to Isaiah 61, quoting the opening verses:

> *The spirit of the Lord God is upon me,*
> *because the Lord has anointed me;*
> *he has sent me to bring good news to the oppressed,*
> *to bind up the brokenhearted,*
> *to proclaim liberty to the captives,*
> *and release to the prisoners;*
> *to proclaim the year of the Lord's favor,*
> *and the day of vengeance of our God;*
> *to comfort all who mourn;*
> *to provide for those who mourn in Zion—*
> *to give them a garland instead of ashes,*
> *the oil of gladness instead of mourning,*
> *the mantle of praise instead of a faint spirit.*

They will be called oaks of righteousness,
the planting of the Lord, to display his glory.[82]

The woman, hearing Elaw quote Isaiah, was astonished. She had mourned, had been brokenhearted, and learned that God wanted to give her good news and heal her. Elaw had spoken the words the woman needed to hear, and the woman responded with praise. Elaw, grateful, claimed the woman as "one of the many of the earliest seals of my ministry in Manchester." The Scripture that Elaw read to the woman was the one Jesus had read when he preached in his hometown of Nazareth in Luke 4. By choosing this Scripture, Elaw aligned herself with Jesus as she preached these words to the woman—Jesus "binds up the broken-hearted," as did she. The woman "glorified God in [Elaw]."

Elaw's Encounters with the English Police

Not everyone Elaw encountered in England doubted her ability to preach, and some especially welcomed her ministry, like the Bryanites, who flourished in Cornwall but also proselytized in London. At the time, the Bryanites were a breakaway sect of Wesleyan Methodists and known for their approval of women ministers.[83] One historian describes them as gathering "classes that might otherwise have never been reached."[84] A friend introduced her to the Bryanite group, which was about ready to hold a service on a street in London. The preacher, upon meeting Elaw, asked her to preach instead. As she began to preach to the Bryanites, a crowd gathered around her, eager to hear a Black woman with an American accent. Seeing the crowd, two police came forward, obviously irritated at this impromptu public church service. They tapped her on the shoulder and asked where she received the authority to preach. A member of the crowd responded in defense of her: "She has her authority in her hand." What he meant by that was the "Word of God"—the Bible.[85] The gathered group left. Elaw does not record the police officers' responses. Despite this encounter, her calling and witness stood firm. She believed in her belovedness even when government authorities would try to tell her otherwise.

At the time of this interaction, the English government was in the middle of organizing a paid police force. The Municipal Corporations Act of 1835 allowed for local governments to assemble and regulate a police presence. The act met much resistance. People were rightly afraid police presence would limit their freedom of speech. Police were poorly equipped, poorly trained, and worked long hours with little pay. These conditions meant that the quality of recruits was low and that they faced resistance from the public.[86] While Elaw worried about how they may restrict her preaching, she also believed that even they could convert and receive salvation. While in Manchester visiting a friend, Elaw encountered a police officer and his wife among the guests visiting. Elaw struck up a conversation with the wife and asked about their faith. The wife remarked that her husband "had been a religious man, but had fallen from grace." She begged Elaw to talk with him. As they began their conversation, "he burst into tears." He described how police officers "were regarded as the offscouring of the human race, and that few cared for their souls." Elaw patiently listened to his story, offering a message of hope found in Christ. He thanked Elaw for coming to him and Elaw, the officer, and his wife prayed together. This moment served as the beginning of Elaw's evangelistic success in Manchester.[87]

Elaw went on to preach over two hundred times in Manchester and the surrounding communities. The rest of Elaw's narrative reads like both a spiritual diary and a travel memoir, detailing with whom she lodged, whom she encountered, and where she preached. She writes, "In heat and cold, through wet and dry weather, by night and day, I laboured in that part of God's vineyard, preaching the gospel of Christ incessantly, wherever opportunity was afforded me."[88] In one instance, she describes how so many people wanted to hear her preach that the venue was overfilled, and hundreds of people had to be turned away.[89] Toward the end of her memoir, she recalls that she preached "considerably more than one thousand sermons," using whatever offerings she received to pay for her travel and ministry.[90] Elaw's ministry, from the camp meetings in the United States to her journeys in England, was like that of the early evangelists in Luke 15, who similarly took no extra supplies and relied upon the goodness of God and the hospitality of those whom she met.

A Gesture toward the Future

Elaw's memoir ends with an exhortation to Christians of all denominations, that they may hold fast to the truth of the gospel, "keeping our faith in continual exercise." Boldly, and perhaps foolishly as a Black woman, she writes of her work, "These humble memoirs will doubtless continue to be read long after I shall cease from my earthly labors and existence."[91] She self-published her memoir in 1846 in London. Her understanding of her uniqueness as a Black woman preacher, along with how her writings could share the gospel more widely than her sermons, sparked her writing. She lived another thirty years after publishing her memoir.

Only in 2021, when Kimberly Blockett published an annotated edition of her *Memoirs*, could Elaw's post-*Memoirs* years be witnessed. Elaw remarried a white Methodist named Ralph Shum in 1851, who died in 1854, leaving Elaw with a small inheritance. She continued to preach throughout England; she even had a chapel built in her honor. According to historical records, she died in 1873 in London at about eighty years old and was buried in an unmarked grave. British obituaries, sadly, did not mention her illustrious preaching career.[92] Her unknowability today may render her foolish to English society, but like she inferred, her theology and stories still inspire and can teach twenty-first-century readers today.

Elaw's Foolish Ministry Fleshed Out

Elaw's whole ministry, including her ministry to England, was considered foolish by many people she encountered. Others, perhaps seen as foolish themselves, took great comfort in Elaw's message. Against England's colonial proselytizing heritage, she asserted that she, and her Black female body, were where God foolishly dwelled.

Liminally Paradoxical

Elaw's liminality allowed her to embrace "foolishness" as a way of life. Her physical body as a Black woman in the nineteenth century rendered her social location as liminal and foolish. To be "liminal" is to be unable to be categorized neatly or to refuse to fit into societal assumptions. What she perceived as God's calling for her conflicted with her position in dominant society. In England, people questioned Elaw's presence as a Black woman, wondering what she could offer them, as they were not able to neatly fit her into any category. As someone deigned "inferior" by white society, she also had wide-reaching success in her ministry, rendering her presence as sort of a paradox. Her liminality implied "ambiguity and paradox, a confusion of all the customary categories."[93] A common definition of a paradox is to hold "a set of mutually inconsistent propositions, each of which seems to be true."[94] Elaw did not shy away from her status as a Black woman evangelist and occasionally saw her race and gender as especially enabling her to preach the gospel. Even though structurally she would have no place, precisely from that place she could clearly see the blind spots and shortcomings of others. Her status allowed her to embrace "foolishness," as it was essential to her calling, and access the divine more clearly.

Zilpha Elaw's (em)bodiment as a Black woman rendered her inherently "foolish" according to the dominant societal norms of her time and place.[95] In the United States, the curse of Ham was thought of as having rendered Black people as afflicted by God and heathens worthy of enslavement. The curse of Ham originates in Genesis in which

Ham, Noah's son, looks upon Noah's nakedness while Noah was drunk. Noah curses him, saying that Ham and his descendants will be the "lowest of slaves" to their siblings. Enslavers and proslavery advocates used the curse to justify enslavement of African American people by white colonizers, a concept that was perpetuated by pastors and government officials alike.[96] Thus Black people, at least according to the dominant white supremacist society of the nineteenth-century United States, were rendered as inherently inferior intellectually compared to their white counterparts.[97] To be Black was to be foolish according to the world.

Compounded with Elaw's Blackness was her identity as a woman. Her narrative records multiple instances of people denying her opportunities to speak and preach on account of her sex.[98] She implies that those around her did not see her as qualified to preach or lead. As a liminal person, Elaw moved beyond and between boundaries enforced by white English Christians, presenting educated arguments for women preaching and proclaiming the foolishness of the cross to those who questioned her presence. Elaw's writing represented a type of "code switching." Elaw, as a Black evangelist, knew how middle- to upper-class white people expected her to act and could massage their egos through complicated rhetoric. Simultaneously she could speak just as effectively with and to people like the police officer or the woman in her home. She perceived this code switch as a gift of her liminality, which was initiated and sustained by the work of the Spirit.[99]

In an example of her appealing to a more literalistic reading of the Bible, Elaw compliments a certain Mrs. G., whom she visited frequently while in Hudersfield. She describes her as "one of the genuine daughters of Sarah; reverent to her husband." Elaw then seems to make what appears today a sexist comment, saying that "high minded and insubordinate wives who profess the religion of Jesus" should be like Mrs. G. and pay attention to their duties as Christian wives. Of course, Elaw wrote this after her own husband died. Still, Elaw and her husband had argued about her own ministry, and so Elaw appears to contradict herself. Here, Elaw appeals to an audience whose interpretation of such strictures was more literal even though she herself had defied her husband by preaching.

Zilpha Elaw's liminality was fertile ground to accept paradox. For many, paradoxes seem beyond the realm of imagination and are considered fantastical or absurd.[100] The presence of paradox looms large in this "foolish" preacher.[101] When Elaw traveled to the southern United States, her liminality as someone who did not fully occupy any space or category was paradoxical. She even mentions the paradox herself. After she tells the enslavers "all the things that they ever did," she remarks, "This was a paradox to them indeed: for they were not deficient of pastors and reverend divines, who possessed all the advantages of talents, learning, respectability, and world influence, to aid their religious efforts; and yet the power of truth and of God was never so manifest in any of their agencies as with the dark coloured female stranger, who had come from afar to minister among them."[102] Alluding to Paul, Elaw describes power as weakness and the despised as uplifted.[103] The outsider, Elaw, is the one who contains the indwelling Spirit. The residents, the enslavers with their learned preachers, do not possess such authority.[104] Elaw feels this paradox within her own person, claiming her "bodily presence" as weak, unsuitable for preaching to large crowds, yet she was "a prodigy" to the people around her in the South. Elaw flaunted her weakness and her solidarity with the enslaved people in establishing her spiritual authority. Here, her foolishness represented wisdom. White people who thought her an oddity respected her as a religious authority, asking her to minister "the word of life" to them.[105]

Theologian Harvey Cox sees the liminality, paradox, and foolishness that characterize Elaw's ministry as inseparable. He suggests that this is the role of court jesters in the medieval period in developing a "theology of juxtaposition" (in other words, a theology of paradox). A court jester functioned as entertainment to the wealthy but also could speak the truth to the powerful in a way regular commoners could not. A theology that "merely sanctifies society or pursues 'relevance' at all costs cannot produce any refreshing juxtaposition." That is, one needs the *viewpoint of liminality* to see clearly. Cox says the jester's role describes this epistemology, claiming one cannot be a jester while occupying an archbishop's role, implying that one *must* be liminal. Further, he outlines this paradoxical liminality as "to 'frequent' good society but not belong to it; to be its 'habitué' and at the same time to observe it from the sidelines—this sounds very much like St. Paul's suggestion that the church should be 'in but not of the world.'"[106] Elaw "frequented" proper society and at times conformed to society but always found herself at the margins because of her social status.

With paradoxical liminality comes danger. Liminality implies an ambiguous phase between two situations or social statuses. Often this in-between space contains potential or actual danger.[107] This danger was present in Elaw's itinerant ministry. In Elaw's case, she knowingly entered the dangerous slaveholding Southern states, facing not only physical danger from slave catchers but spiritual danger. She describes Satan as distressing "[her] soul with the fear of being arrested and sold for a slave, which their laws would have warranted." In a small town, where most Black people were probably enslaved, she described the intense fear of immediate arrest, where she prayed to Jesus for relief. As she traveled to England alone without knowing anyone, she willingly put herself in danger and into the mercy of God.

Hopefully Tricksterish

Zilpha Elaw embodied the motif of a hopeful trickster. A trickster, a figure often found in Afrodiasporic traditions, is a "holy fool" who, in the face of despair or cynicism, practices "persistent hope against all odds."[108] Elaw embraced an almost nagging doggedness in her memoir: she knew God called her, and no one could stop her. As a hopeful trickster, she continued to minister to people who rejected her, often exposing their evils in the process.

For instance, she realized her audience was mostly white, middle-class British and attempted to appeal to their egos. When describing her ministry in Salem, Massachusetts, she explains to her audience as an aside, "I hope to be forgiven by my English brethren in saying, that it is not an uncommon thing for white Christians to [condemn] the morals of their [Black siblings] without an adequate occasion."[109] Since white people were from the "more cultivated Saxon stock," a higher standard of Christianity was expected from them. She employs complicated verbiage and rhetoric in this direct address, assuming their "superior" Christian morality connected to a higher level of education. She writes in this style, however, to demonstrate that while white people expressed "high-toned sensibility and civilization," those "more polished Christians" possessed the most "immoral and debasing" attributes of "covetousness and worldly pride." Elaw slyly remarks, "These vices have unrestrained course throughout the more civilized Christian communities." To get rid of these sins "would fill [the church] with confusion, and crumble to ruins every denominational superstructure in Christendom."[110] The sins of the "civilized" white leadership pervaded the church to such an extent that if these people were exposed or dismissed, there would be no church structure or hierarchy.

As a foolish trickster, Elaw discerned her context, and by appealing to white notions of civility through a more complicated writing style, she could criticize such civility for being empty of faith. She probably knew these comments would engender criticism or rejection by the persons to whom she appealed; simultaneously, in her hopeful trickster mentality, she exposed white people as having shallow faith and exposed the dominant religious institutions as full of corruption.[111] By embracing a more complicated rhetoric, she could (in a trickster-like fashion) both appeal to and criticize white sensibilities without white people necessarily knowing it. Her tricksterish behavior demonstrated a hope in herself: though considered foolish by the outside world, she shamed the wise.[112]

Wonderfully Interruptive

Elaw's foolish charisma interrupted the status quo. Her interruptive presence evoked wonder within herself and provoked others to wonder at and with her. As a foolish preacher, she was an "agent of interruption." Her preaching disturbed and disrupted what was considered normal; cracking enshrined and apparently static structures.[113] As a Black woman itinerant traveling to the United States and England, Elaw failed to fit into the category deemed fit by polite white society.

In Zilpha Elaw's case, those around her deemed her preaching presence and authority unusual, strange, an oddity, and as a foolishness to entertain rather than an authority to trust. Her way of being in the world disrupted and defied expectations. When the church becomes comfortable in its authority or power, preaching fools expose its power as false or corrupt.[114] Elaw "subverted dominant paradigms of authority," creating "alternative meanings and truths," and resisting anything that would limit her freedom.[115] Elaw as an "agent of interruption" created an "alternative meaning" by claiming her Christ-likeness, implicitly associating herself with both Paul and Jesus in her travels around the United States and England. In this sense, her interruptive presence provoked wonder in others.

For example, while in Portland, Maine, Elaw felt a prompting to go to the more remote town of Bath. She expresses hesitation about this calling, as she "received no invitation," knew no one, and had heard "the town was not inhabited by one person of colour." She asked the church there if she could preach, stating, "This was the first time in my life that I had ever requested as a favour to myself." She received a tepid response from the people, who said they had never heard of her, but she was welcome to attend their prayer meeting. When she approached the location of the prayer meeting, the woman who greeted her affirmed it was the correct place but suggested Elaw go to the friend who had sent her. Irritated, Elaw departed, trying to find anyone who knew about her coming. No one did. Elaw reluctantly returned to the prayer meeting house, and the same woman cracked the door open, only to begin to shut it in Elaw's face. Elaw opened it and found it full of pastors and a congregation ready for a prayer meeting. In her memoir, she ponders the rude reception and wonders why God called her there.[116]

One of the preachers approached her before the service, saying, "Sister, I suppose you wish to address the meeting," claiming the group wanted to listen to this woman whom they had never heard of before. As she preached, she writes, "the Lord was with me in the work" and "much feeling was excited and many tears were shed."[117] In this moment, Elaw understood why God wanted her to preach, even after receiving such a cool reception.

Elaw knew beforehand that her presence as a Black woman in Bath, Maine, would provoke curiosity and derision. Her expectations were met by the rude reception of the prayer meeting's hostess and the initial indifference of the congregation. However, her interruption provoked awe in both the congregation and her. The congregation begged her to stay for a while, moved by her preaching. After she fulfilled other preaching obligations, she returned to Bath, where she preached to "a very large and attentive audience" who took up a love offering on her behalf. She remarked it was a "larger sum than [she] had received from any other congregation in the State of Maine." She seemed to be in a wonderful state of shock: "Although my reception was so rude and repulsive at the first, yet my way was enlarged, my messaged welcomed, and my subsequent treatment warmly cordial and affectionate."[118] Elaw contemplated God's wonderful goodness in the generous reception of the very same people who slammed the door in her face. Her interruption into their space provoked the wonder of the congregation, and of herself, at God's providence.

Zilpha Elaw's ministry indicates a foolish mentality that celebrates her attributes and identity, which others would shame. Elaw's skin color and sex allowed her to uniquely share truths with powerful people who would otherwise dignify her as less than human. Her paradoxical liminality enabled her to be hopefully tricksterish, which in turn enabled her to wonderfully interrupt a dominant society, allowing her audience to glimpse a God whose love is abundantly foolish. God prefers the outcasts whose gifts are overlooked as messengers for God—as Elaw demonstrates.

Elaw saved her most incisive and prophetic critiques for those with power: the enslavers, English Methodist ministers who denied her right to preach, and middle- to upper-class women who hosted prayer meetings. In this sense, she punched up. The term *punching up* is used frequently in comedy; comedians who "punch up" target the privileged, those "who are insulated from harmful real-world effects that might result from their humor."[119] This punching up applies to Elaw's focus of critique on those more powerful than her, as well as her foolish preaching. She grounded the punching up in Scripture. As Mitzi Smith explains, "Black female preachers used 'biblical reversal,' grounded in biblical radicalism, to turn ideas of socio-political inequality and male authority on its head."[120] As she punched up, Elaw followed the path of Jesus and Paul—demonstrating how power will be made perfect in weakness and the meek shall inherit the earth.[121]

Elaw's witness emphasized that foolish preaching is pneumatologically rooted. She could be pneumatologically rooted—grounded in the Holy Spirit—because she was forced into a liminal space based on her race and gender. Preaching fools are "agents of the Spirit," "reopening the liminal space between the cross and resurrection," invoking new and disturbing paradigms.[122] Her conversion and sanctification are marked by the Spirit's movement, and throughout her memoir, she discerns the Spirit's promptings as she traveled, ministered, and contemplated. The Spirit took her to places where she experienced rejection, such as having the door slammed in her face. She relied on the Spirit's sustenance when she experienced heaviness and doubt in her ministry. She contrasted hegemonic common sense—"self-sufficient reason"—with the Spirit's foolish work. The Spirit's irruption still collides with common sense today when it is pneumatologically rooted.

Conclusion: Keep Faith a Continual Exercise

At the conclusion of her *Memoirs*, Elaw warned her British audience to hold firm, "keeping [their] faith in continual exercise."[123] Elaw's stubborn foolishness held throughout her life as she exercised her faith. From her insistence on the truthfulness of her vision, including the cow bowing in the stall, to her going back to the woman who slammed the door in her face and eventually preaching to the gathered group, Elaw's foolish wisdom contested dominant understandings of Christianity that were tied to white concepts of what was proper or civil. As she articulated her theology through her *Memoirs*, she presented herself as a Christlike figure whose paradoxical liminality enabled her to minister to people from all walks of life. As she ministered, she interrupted people's popular conceptions of what faith should look like and instead depicted a Christ not concerned with the wisdom of the world but offering a power made perfect in weakness. Her memoir and ministry laid bare what such power looked like and acted like. Power was not found in the wealthy or among white society but in the ministry of a Black itinerant woman.

3

Julia Foote
Bodying the Word

Be not kept in bondage by those who say, "We suffer not a woman to teach," thus quoting Paul's words, but not rightly applying them. What though we are called to pass through deep waters, so our anchor is cast within the veil, both sure and steadfast! Blessed experience!

—Julia Foote

Julia Foote heard various prohibitions of her ministry throughout her life. Toward the end of her autobiography, *A Brand Plucked from the Fire: An Autobiographical Sketch*, she addresses women directly, arguing that they should not listen to those who quote the apostle Paul's injunction against women preaching in order to wield unhealthy power and authority. Foote, the first woman deacon and second woman elder in the African Methodist Episcopal Zion Church, practiced a style of biblical exegesis that celebrated her humanity and the humanity of the people to whom she ministered. In her preface, she describes her primary audience as her "own race," unlike Zilpha Elaw, who wrote to a primarily white British audience. Foote's preface indicates her hope that "many—especially of [her] own race—may be led to believe and enter into rest." In that phrase, she references the rest promised by God to the faithful in Hebrews 4:3. Perhaps, knowing that her African American siblings often received no rest from white supremacy, she especially wanted to emphasize that "sweet soul rest" as being known, loved, and called by God.[1] Throughout her autobiography, she expands the notions of both "Word" and "body." She reflected the cadence of Scripture in her writing, in addition to using public documents from her world, to share the gospel. She theologized using Scripture and current events to offer a prophetic declaration on the God who sanctified her to bring good news to others. Her calling was to help people say yes to God by bodying the Word of God to them.

How Julia Foote Bodied the Word

Foote organized her "autobiographical sketch"[2] differently than Zilpha Elaw did her *Memoirs*. While Zilpha Elaw's prose is long, reading as a travel memoir like the book of Acts,[3] Foote arranged her *Sketch* into chapters. The chapters are short, usually centering around a particular event.

They sometimes include an exhortation, call to action, or warning at the end. Put simply, Foote writes like a preacher would preach, addressing her audience directly, switching between narrative and sermonizing. Thus, for her, to body the Word is to express herself as a sermonic event and established spiritual authority.

Bodying the Word

Julia Foote "bodies" or "enfleshes" the Word, implying that her body is a sacred carrier of the Word. The human experience always includes a body. Thus, *bodying the Word* contests the dualism that "embody" implicitly suggests.[4] To body the Word specifically is to claim that bodies engaged in the act of proclamation are holy, sacred bodies. Bodying the Word is analogous to womanist theologian M. Shawn Copeland's theological anthropology in that she focuses on the lives of Black women to demonstrate particularity without essentialization; to show self-transcendence without self-forgetting.[5] Copeland's emphasis on the body serving as a place for divine revelation where both theology and praxis coalesce is displayed through the words of Julia Foote throughout her autobiography, and particularly in how she bodied the Word in her sanctification.

The idea of bodying also connotes fluidity and activeness. Bodies constantly move—even lying down requires the motion of breath, heart, and lungs. Thus, to use the phrase *bodying the Word* implicates dynamic action in the Word itself. A word is not stagnant on a page but can only have life when attached to a body. This holds true theologically and biblically. The Word becoming flesh in the prologue in John's Gospel is similar to the Word becoming "bodied." John 1:14 proclaims, "The Word became flesh and lived among us." With her body as a site of divine revelation, Foote wrote and preached ordinary words to point to the Word. If body is conceived as dynamic, Word should be also. A slippage or movement occurs as Foote used her words to describe the Word, whether the Word is understood as Scripture or the revelation of Jesus the Christ. In the way Foote engaged in Scripture and public documents, ambiguity and paradox are necessarily present in the incarnation of words.[6] As Foote bodied the Word, she wove together Scripture, personal anecdotes, and public memory to show both God's saving work and how God called her as a holy prophet.

Biblical Depictions of Bodying the Word

Prophets in the Bible revealed something about God's character and humanity's relationship to God. At times, to body the Word meant one was chosen. In Genesis 15, Abram received a word from the Lord in a vision that he would have as many descendants as the stars in the sky. He internalized that Word, trusting God even though he was an old man. In other instances, to body the Word was to be a mediator between the people and God. In Exodus 24, Moses was the only person allowed near God. He communicated the words of the Lord to the people. The prophet Ezekiel took a literal approach to bodying the Word: the Lord told Ezekiel to eat a scroll and then prophesy to Israel.[7] After Ezekiel physically ate the scroll, God told him that he would be able to speak what God commanded.

God warned Ezekiel that even while he was authorized to speak on God's behalf, the people may still reject or ignore his message. Ezekiel's physical presence became associated with God's presence for the Hebrew people. For Ezekiel, bodying the Word by physically eating the scroll gave him the strength to preserve in a difficult setting, as God made his forehead "like the hardest stone" against the stubborn Israelites, who would, at times, not listen to him.[8] Bodying the Word strengthened Ezekiel to persevere despite the Hebrews' stubbornness.

The New Testament continued the tradition of Hebrew prophets bodying the Word of God to the community.[9] In the Gospels, John the Baptist bodied the words of Isaiah 40 in his prophetic declarations: "In the wilderness prepare the way of the Lord, make straight in the desert a highway for our God."[10] All four Gospel writers point to John the Baptist as bodying these words: preaching repentance, baptizing, and making people aware of the coming Messiah Jesus. John the Baptist's preaching indicated God's presence was near. While John did not eat the scroll like Ezekiel, the description Gospel writers give him indicates he is a prophet akin to those in the Old Testament. For instance, Matthew's Gospel describes him as wearing "clothing of camel's hair with a leather belt around his waist, and his food was locusts and wild honey."[11] This echoes 2 Kings 1:8, where the prophet Elijah is described as wearing "a garment of hair and had a leather belt around his waist."[12] Matthew, along with the other Gospel writers, describes John as a prophet who bodies a Word of repentance and salvation to his community. John the Baptist's prophetic utterances pointed to *the* Word, Jesus Christ.

John told the people, "One who is more powerful than I is coming after me; I am not worthy to carry his sandals. He will baptize you with the Holy Spirit and fire."[13] Julia Foote took up this mantle in preaching repentance and leading her audience toward salvation, using her words to point to the Word who is Jesus. In this way, Foote's bodying the Word followed the lineage of the biblical prophets.

Bodying the Word Connecting to the Doctrine of Revelation

Julia Foote's bodying the Word does not extend to Scripture alone. She embraced the concept of *Word* as holding multiple meanings. The twentieth-century theologian Karl Barth's concept of *revelation* illuminates a more nuanced understanding of *Word*. For Barth, revelation is foundational to understanding the threefold Word of God. Besides the Word incarnate, the other two forms are Scripture, which "bears witness to past revelation," and proclamation, which "promises future revelation."[14] Proclamation and Scripture exist as forms of the Word of God only to the extent that they are caught up in the event of God's revelation. And "revelation in fact does not differ from the person of Jesus Christ nor from the reconciliation accomplished in Him."[15] His concept of Word as "living" connects to the living Word—Jesus Christ.[16] For Barth, *Word* always already implied dynamism, incarnation, and Christology.[17]

Foote depicts the Word in an active, dynamic manner that is "enfleshed." Included in this "enfleshment" is the connection between Spirit and Word. In this sense, bodying the Word affirms the active dynamism of Word and the implications of what can be considered inspired. The Spirit inspires ordinary words, which in turn point to the Word who is Christ Jesus.

Julia Foote's Unique Way of Bodying the Word

Julia Foote engages not only Scripture but also political contemporary writings to assert herself as a Black preacher called by God. Paradoxically, at times, she seems critical of reading the newspaper or sources other than the Bible. For instance, in addressing parents on how to foster their children's spirituality, she asks, "Are [the children] at home reading books or newspapers that corrupt the heart, bewilder the mind, and lead down to the bottomless pit?"[18] To be fair, in Foote's era, white people wrote and published the most newspapers. They often depicted Black Americans unfairly and applied racist tropes. Newspapers often stereotyped Black people by giving them an exaggerated dialect and not letting them speak for themselves, depicting them instead as illiterate and exoticized.[19] Despite Foote's reticence to read newspapers, she knew about current events that were reported in newspapers, pamphlets, and other documents.

Julia Foote utilized rhetoric from "national sociopolitical debates" to write her sketch so that it was not only a spiritual autobiography but activist in nature.[20] By way of her personal experience, she offered a larger commentary on white America's treatment of Black people, and Black women in particular.[21] Thus Foote perceived particular events in her world as having theological significance. Her bodiment of the Word implied that God cared and had something to say about such current events. By sprinkling snippets of these public documents throughout her text, she implicitly suggests that the theological is political, and the political is theological. By including such public documents alongside scriptural cadences and references, she highlights the necessity of loving and witnessing to God in all of one's body, soul, and mind. In addition, she intends for her experience to console her Black siblings. Because they could identify with her, they could find comfort in her message.

Richard Allen's Autobiography

Foote's first engagement with a publicly known text occurs in the very first chapter of her autobiography as she details her parents' early life before she was born. Her father was born as a freed person, but as a child, he was kidnapped from his parents and enslaved. Her mother was born enslaved in New York State. Her mother's enslaver severely abused her. Once, after her mother's enslaver beat her, "he washed her quivering back with strong salt water." She then was instructed to wear a rough linen shirt, which stuck to her wounds.[22] Foote's father, who as an enslaved person drove a team of horses, was constantly exposed to the harsh New York winters. Her parents purchased their freedom as adults, married, and had Julia's older sister. One night, after returning home from a dance, her parents attempted to cross a swollen stream. Her mother, holding her baby, almost drowned. After that harrowing incident, Foote's parents "made a public profession of religion and united with the Methodist Episcopal Church."[23]

At the time they joined the church, an increasing number of Black people were attending white Methodist Episcopal churches. In those churches, Black people sat in segregated areas away from the chancel during worship services. Foote described the racism her parents endured in their first Methodist church: "They were not treated as Christian believers, but as poor lepers. They were obliged to occupy certain seats in one corner of the gallery, and dared not come down to partake of the Holy Communion until the last white communicant had left the table."[24]

A particular instance her parents recounted left an impression upon Foote. One Sunday at that church, Foote's mother and friend got up to receive communion after they thought all the white people finished. They did not see the "poorer classes of whites" and were stopped by a "mother of Israel" (a fellow African American woman) who said, "Don't you know better than to go to the table when white folks are there?"[25] Foote explains that this inequality at the communion table was one "of the fruits of slavery." The church's attitude was not of the Holy Spirit, for under the Holy Spirit, all are considered equal. Rather, the congregation was "deluded by a spirit of error, which says to the poor and [Black] ones among them: 'Stand back a little—I am holier than thou.'"[26]

In telling this story, Foote alludes to Richard Allen's autobiography.[27] Richard Allen founded the African Methodist Episcopal Church after he and his fellow African Americans were treated with disdain at the white-led St. George's Methodist Episcopal Church in Philadelphia. One Sunday morning, Allen and his friends went to their usual section at church, "not knowing any better." As the congregation prayed, white leaders roughly pulled up the Black Rev. Absalom Jones because he was sitting where white people wanted to sit. Jones, eyes closed, was deep in worshipful prayer at the time. Though he begged the white leaders to wait until after he finished praying, the white leaders called for additional assistance to forcibly remove Jones from his seat. After this incident, Allen remarked that he, Jones, and the other Black worshippers "all went out of the church in a body," adding, "They were no more plagued with us in the church."[28] This story, in part, marked the creation of the African Methodist Episcopal Church, a safe haven where Black people could worship freely.

By alluding to Allen's narrative, Foote establishes herself in the "lineage" of leaders in the early African Methodist Episcopal Church.[29] Allen's story was the story of her denominational heritage. Her audience would have known Allen's history and noticed the connection. Thus she offers an example of bodying the Word that isn't bodying Scripture directly. By alluding to Allen's autobiography in her own, Foote places herself on similar footing to Allen. She connects her life to his public memory, legitimizing her calling in the process. She also lays the foundation to adopt a similar prophetic impetus as Allen. After Allen and the other parishioners left, they founded a new Methodist denomination that fully celebrated Black people. Allen refused to return to St. George's church, even after its leaders met with him on multiple occasions and threatened excommunication. He also was determined that the new church that he and those parishioners built in 1793, what he called the first Black church in the United States, would remain Methodist in character and be a place where Black people could freely preach and worship without the interference of the white Methodist Episcopal Church.[30] Like Allen, Foote's dictations of where and how she preached would prophetically stand against a white supremacist and misogynist culture.

Learning from both her mother's and Richard Allen's experiences, later in her *Sketch*, Foote would always insist on ensuring that whatever pulpit she occupied, she would be fully welcomed. In turn, she confirms safety for all people by demanding there be no restrictions on who could enter the sanctuary and where they could sit. By loving and advocating for herself, she simultaneously advocates and loves her neighbors, particularly her Black neighbors. Her purposeful reversal of Richard Allen's experience testifies to how she deployed her spiritual authority for freedom. In showing the failures of the churches that put limitations on her preaching and alluding to Allen's autobiography, she sets the stage for her ministry to be just as valuable and in the theological heritage as Allen and the creation of the African Methodist Episcopal Church. She bodies Allen's story and adapts it to her parents' own experience.

John Van Patten

While her parents taught her some basic prayers and encouraged her faith, Julia Foote recalls having her first "religious impression" at eight years old while attending a "big meeting" with her parents at church. This meeting appeared to be a revival. Two ministers from that meeting came to Foote's home. One of them, who "had long gray hair and a beard," asked her if she prayed. Frightened, thinking the minister was Jesus, she told him yes. He then began to pray over her, "long and loud." After the men left, Foote's mother came to her. She told her the man was not Jesus and began to encourage Foote to pray often, for her faith would save her. Foote followed her mother's orders, taking immense joy in learning new prayers, like the Lord's Prayer.[31] She took the prayers she had been taught as a child and bodied their words as her own.

Not long after the ministers visited her house, Foote asked her father if he could teach her the letters of the alphabet so she could read the Bible. He replied, "Child, I hardly know them myself." He had wanted to send his children to school, but no schools in the area would accept Black children. Nonetheless, with significant effort, he taught Foote the alphabet. Reflecting back on that time, Foote remarks, "The children of the present time, taught at five years of age, can not realize my joy at being able to say the entire alphabet when I was nine years old."[32] Looking back, she understood that her ability to read Scripture would later enable her to body the Word in her ministry.

While her parents had limited education, they pushed for Julia Foote to be educated. At ten years old, they sent her to live with a white family—the Primes, "who had no children"—in a servant type of arrangement. Foote, like Zilpha Elaw in the previous chapter, performed chores for this family in exchange for room and board. (This, of course, could be construed as enslavement by a different name.) Foote explains, "[The Primes] soon became quite fond of me. I really think Mrs. Prime loved me."[33] Living with the Primes enabled her to go to a country school. Foote took to school with eagerness, and her desire to read the Bible meant she quickly learned how to spell and read. Her desire for holiness required learning to study and read the Scriptures.

Foote's time with the Primes set the scene for her to be able to include a story that did not actually happen to her. She uses the narrative to explain her views about the promise of redemption found in Christ and capital punishment. As she relays in her autobiography, Foote describes how John Van Patten,[34] whom she identifies as her teacher, had been dating a woman who told him her friend thought him rather unsmart. Van Patten, enraged, sought out the offending woman and shot her in the presence of her children. On his way to turn himself in to the authorities, he encountered the dead woman's husband and told him what he had done. Van Patten then surrendered himself to be taken into custody. He was tried, found guilty, and sentenced to hanging. While imprisoned, the widower of the woman Van Patten murdered visited his jail cell, praying that he would be converted to Christianity before his death. The widower's prayer prompted Van Patten to seek God in earnest, and for two weeks in his cell, he prayed and cried and begged for salvation. On February 1, a month before his execution, Van Patten "felt [his burden] removed": "I felt that my sins were forgiven: I loved the children of God and could pray for my enemies."[35] Foote inserts herself in the story, depicting herself as witnessing the hanging with horror along with the rest of the townspeople. She later describes nightmares where she saw his head rolling around on the floor. At the end of that chapter, she exhorts her readers to pray that the government abolish the death penalty.[36]

Taking a step back, Foote was most likely not present at the execution. While Van Patten lived in Schenectady, New York, where she was born, Foote would have been only two years old when Van Patten was hung. Nonetheless, the story still lurked in residents' minds decades later, when she composed her *Sketch*. The 1825 pamphlet, *The Trial and Life and Confessions of John F. Van Patten*, which depicted his trial, conversion, and death, was portrayed as a "cautionary tale of a sinful life juxtaposed against the saving power of Jesus."[37] Indeed, the end of the pamphlet describes his last words, which were of a hymn expressing his trust in God. While Foote may not have witnessed *this* hanging, she likely witnessed *a* public hanging during her childhood. By choosing to associate the hanging she experienced with the well-circulated pamphlet, she adds validity to her insistence that God could redeem murderers, and the death penalty as it stood in the United States was contrary to God's abundant grace.[38]

Julia Foote probably did not see the inclusion of this event in her autobiography as lying, even though she did not know Van Patten personally. Here, she bodies the words in the pamphlet by undergirding public events (like Van Patten's hanging) with Scripture. As she reflects upon the hanging, she recalls both Old Testament and New Testament Scriptures. She recalls the Scripture from Deuteronomy 19:21 and Exodus 21:23, which say, "Life for life." This Scripture, she notes, is what "many believe God commands." But, Foote affirms, Jesus gave a new commandment. Christians are to love one another and resist retaliation by turning the other cheek.[39] Jesus, as he hung upon the cross, prayed to God, "Father, forgive them, for they know not what they do."[40] Christians, she suggests, should follow the example of Jesus, not seeking revenge, but instead choosing love.[41]

The emphasis on love, and her rejection of revenge in the form of the death penalty, compelled Foote to include this story in her memoir. As Foote bodies the Scripture and alludes to the pamphlet, a slippage occurs of what is real, and readers are compelled to examine what is true. For her, Christians approach the question of real and true in several ways. For instance, many Christians question the literal narrative of God creating the world in six twenty-four-hour days in light of evolutionary science or whether Jonah really lived in the belly of the whale for six days. Even if those events did not happen literally as written in Scripture, it does not mean they do not contain truth. Stories tell truths even if they themselves are not factually accurate. As Jocelyn Moody writes, the genre of autobiography, in some sense "fictionalizes reality." She continues, "The 'fictions' of black personal narratives are rooted in the 'facts' in the subjects' lives . . . Then, as now, black people understood all too well the European American suspicion of their veracity."[42] By incorporating the Van Patten pamphlet into her own narrative, and utilizing Scripture to offer a moral judgment, she theologizes that to believe in a God who chose crucifixion rather than revenge was to reject the death penalty.

While she may not have literally observed Van Patten's death, she knew that when his execution occurred, religious and political leaders had been leading a charge to ban capital punishment from at least the turn of the nineteenth century. Most notably, Benjamin Rush, a physician who signed the Declaration of Independence and helped Richard Allen raise money for the first Black church, published his views against capital punishment, which were rooted in his Christian faith.[43] Rush remarks, in 1792, "The punishment of murder by death, is contrary to divine revelation. A religion which commands us to forgive and even to do good to our enemies, can never authorise the punishment of murder by death."[44] Rush's comments paved the way for other anti–death penalty movements to arise. The most popular anti–death penalty literature, written by the universalist minister Charles Spear in 1845, depicted the death penalty as "wholly subversive of any good, and entirely contrary to the spirit of Christianity."[45] Foote knew these Christian arguments against the death penalty and saw herself in line with that theological heritage.

Moreover, Foote, as a Black woman writing fifty-four years after Van Patten's death took place, knew the evil history of lynching, or extralegal executions of Black people by white people before and after the Civil War. In 1820, 85 percent of the Black population in New York, where she lived, were freed persons, while 25 percent, mostly in Dutch rural areas, remained enslaved.[46] Even the freed Black persons did not get the same legal protections as their white counterparts. Because white people did not consider Black people fully human in 1825, white people could quite literally get away with murdering enslaved and freed Black people. Both Frederick Douglass's and Sojourner Truth's memoirs, for instance, depict several instances where

Black people were murdered by white people, sometimes, under the guise of the law. When Black people even got the chance for a trial, the laws, created by propertied white men, proved unfair nor impartial. Julia Foote understood this reality. She also knew that only God could adequately judge and punish people and that God's grace meant that God's people too must be gracious. Therefore, she saw the abolition of the death penalty as a religious, social, and political movement, intended to save both Black and white lives and point to the only hope that is found in Christ. She incorporates Van Patten's story because many in her audience could identify with the cruelty of the criminal justice system of the 1800s and would resonate with her line of thinking. By including Van Patten's story in her own autobiography, she demonstrates that her theology connects with social justice and the concerns of the present world. Bodying the words of the Van Patten pamphlet and bodying the Word, which is Scripture, she could point to the Word incarnate.

A Brand Plucked from the Burning

After a couple of years with the Primes, Foote returned to her parents' home to help care for her younger siblings. She resumed attending the African Methodist Episcopal Church with her family. While drawn to the tenets of the Christian faith, as a burgeoning teenager, she felt the attraction to the pleasures of the world. The lure of parties, drinking, and dancing conflicted with the teachings of her Methodist church.[47]

Her parents' attention had turned to her troubled older sister, and Foote felt free to attend parties. The one time she tried dancing, she felt "a heavy hand" pulling her from the dance floor, causing her to fall. The partygoers rushed around her, concerned about her well-being. She realized the heavy hand came from God, telling her not to dance. When she relayed the information to the crowd, they laughed, calling her "a little Methodist fool." Embarrassed, she attempted to join the dancing again, when the same heavy hand took hold of her, along with a voice commanding her, "Repent! Repent!" She immediately went to her chair and sank to her seat. Her companions again crowded around her, but this time no one mocked her. Instead, the party quietly broke up, stunned by Foote's behavior. When relaying this incident in her memoir, she used the phrase that would become a refrain throughout her work and the title of her memoir: she was "a brand plucked from the burning," saved from sin.[48]

A "brand plucked from the burning" or "a brand plucked from the fire" came from the Old Testament book of Zechariah. In chapter 3, Zechariah saw a vision of the "high priest Joshua" standing before Satan, which in Hebrew means "adversary" or "accuser." While biblical scholars today would probably use the term *accuser*, Foote, whose translation of Scripture was the King James Version, understands him as a person, Satan.[49] Satan was preparing to accuse the high priest Joshua, dressed in filthy rags. Before Satan could get ready to level the accusation, the Lord exclaimed, "The Lord rebuke you, O Satan! The Lord who has chosen Jerusalem rebuke you! Is not this man a brand plucked from the fire?"[50] Then Joshua's rags were replaced with finer clothing, and his sin was removed. An angel of the Lord told him, "If you will walk in my ways and keep [the Lord's] requirements, then you shall rule my house and have charge of my courts, and I will give you the right of access among those who are standing here."[51] The Lord insinuated Joshua would have the authority to lead his community, provided he followed God's ways. The book offers a passing reference to hospitality dependent on success: if Joshua followed God, he would get to invite other leaders "under [his] vine and fig tree."[52] Foote saw God's grace toward the priest Joshua within herself—though Satan was ready to destroy her, God rescued her and chose her to preach and minister. Because of God's grace, she could invite others to experience God's saving presence.

Foote purposefully chooses to use the image of a "brand plucked from the burning," most likely understanding the history behind such usage. She knew people would be familiar with the image and knew its history of association with American itinerant evangelists. As early as 1739, the white Calvinist Anglican preacher George Whitefield described Jesus as having plucked him as a brand out of the burning, "and is continuing to comfort me on every side."[53] The phrase "a brand plucked from the fire" was also one utilized by John Wesley, one of the founders of Methodism, to orient his life. In reflecting upon how he was rescued from a burning building at age six, he and his family understood this miracle as being "plucked from the burning"—quite literally. His family understood this to mean also that Wesley had divine purposes in his vocation—God saved him from the fire for something else.[54] He continued to deploy the brand metaphor throughout his life. When Wesley lay deathly ill in his early fifties, he wrote out his own epitaph:

"Here lieth the Body of John Wesley, a Brand plucked out of the Burning."[55] Wesley would eventually recover and live another thirty years, grounding his identity on that metaphor.

Foote, a member of the African Methodist Episcopal Zion Church in the Wesleyan heritage, penned her autobiography in the embers of the Second Great Awakening in 1879. Foote purposefully adopted the term to associate with both religious authority and revival, firming her place as a religious leader. For Whitefield, Wesley, and Foote, the notion of the "brand plucked from the burning" referred to salvation, solely dependent upon God's grace and being "saved from the flames of sin and death." Simultaneously, for Foote, to be "plucked from the burning" also meant having a place set aside for her ministry, as she could brand others for salvation.[56]

More than one hundred years after Wesley's and Whitefield's deaths, and living with the memories of slavery and the Civil War, Foote's social location as a Black woman allowed her to expand on the notion of "brand." Foote knew the evils of slavery because her parents and others around her told her stories. Literal brands, such as the ones used to mark livestock, were often used to identify enslaved peoples, who bore the branding scars upon their flesh. As Jennifer McFarlane Harris highlights, by evoking the metaphor of "brand," Foote uses a punishment tool—an evil tool—as an indication of chosenness.[57] Her people would no longer be identified by their scars as those who'd been enslaved and tortured but as those destined for salvation, called for a special purpose.

Not long after God's hand fell upon her on the dance floor, Foote frames her conversion story with the metaphor of branding, recalling the events in vivid detail. At age fifteen, after a Sunday night church meeting, she agonizes over the Scripture preached: "And they sung as it were a new song before the throne."[58] She reflected over these words—could she, a sinner, sing a new song? She understood she could not and, her soul despairing, fell into an altered state, continually bothered by a nagging voice that told her she was not worthy to sing. As she lay in her altered state, she did not recognize anyone but seemed to be "walking in the dark." Finally, she cried, "'Lord, have mercy on me, a poor sinner!' The voice which had been crying in my ears ceased at once, and a ray of light flashed across my eyes, accompanied by a sound of far distant singing; the light grew brighter and brighter, and the singing more distinct, and soon I caught the words: 'This is the new song redeemed, redeemed!'" Foote, finally, could sing that new song. In mystical terms, she recalls, "I was billed with rapture too deep for words. Was I not indeed a brand plucked from the burning?"[59] Here, she describes her branding as something for God's purpose, just like the high priest Joshua in the book of Zechariah.

Immediately after her conversion, she jumped headlong into her faith, reading the Bible into the night on such a frequent basis that her mother had to take it away from her. She had heard people speak of the doctrine of holiness, otherwise known as sanctification. Methodists viewed entire sanctification as connected with a second blessing that followed conversion. John Wesley, one of Methodism's founders, described sanctification as "the last and highest state of *perfection* in this life. For then are the faithful born again in the full and perfect sense."[60] When Foote inquired about how she may be sanctified as a young woman, her parents brushed her questions aside. Only an older person could achieve sanctification. Nevertheless, she sought sanctification, finding and dialoguing with persons who had already experienced it. Eventually, an older saint (someone who had already experienced sanctification) came to Foote, encouraging her as they examined the Scriptures together. After "that pilgrim's visit," Foote's "large desire was granted," and in that moment, she felt "the weight of glory resting on [her]": "[God] hath plucked me as a brand from the burning, and sealed me unto eternal life." She did not have to search for sanctification; she now "had the full assurance of it."[61] Her experience and description of sanctification furthered her authority to preach and speak for God. The Bible, which had not made sense prior, now became easier to interpret. At the end of her memoir, she describes Christian perfection—also known as entire sanctification—as "not a state of angelic perfection" but "an extinction of every temper contrary to love."[62] Here, she alludes to John Wesley's *Plain Account of Christian Perfection*; even though she may not have read it, she had learned from its teachings. Wesley writes, "By perfection I mean the humble, gentle, patient love of God, and our neighbour, ruling our tempers, words, and actions. I do not include an impossibility of falling from it, either in part or in whole."[63] Having received entire sanctification, she could speak on behalf of God with God's gentle love ruling her temper, word, and action. She bodied Wesley's words in her own experience to demonstrate herself as called and holy.

After Foote received entire sanctification, still many around her doubted that she could serve in a religious leadership role because of her young age. Her pastor came to her home and addressed her deepened faith, hoping to change her mind. He told her that she was "too young" to receive entire sanctification and that "many in the church [were] dissatisfied" with her behavior. The teenaged Foote retorted, "My dear minister, I wish they would all go to Jesus, in prayer and faith, and he will teach them as he has taught me." Upon reflection, she tells her readers, "Though my gifts were but small, I could not be shaken by what man might think or say," because the Lord had blessed her. Overwhelmed with God's favor, she exclaims, "[God] snatched me as a brand from the burning, even me, a poor, ignorant girl!" Here, Foote defied what her minister and her congregation thought. She had experienced sanctification, was cleansed from sin, and wanted others to know the power of Jesus in their lives. Though young, she realized that "God is no respecter of persons."[64] That moment was one of her first instances of saying no to anyone who looked down on her. For her, being a brand plucked from the burning meant becoming saved from sin and branded (sanctified) for ministry. To be branded was to body the Word.

An Unholy Partnership: Foote's Marriage

Julia Foote saw her sanctification tested when she met and married her husband. George Foote had joined the church she attended. Not long afterward, he asked her to marry him. She struggled with his proposal. While he agreed with her that sanctification and holiness were something to be sought, he had not yet experienced them for himself. Foote wanted her marriage to be an equal spiritual partnership, which meant he had to receive sanctification. While courting, he had to leave New York to go to Boston to work. As George and Foote corresponded via mail during that time period, Foote was insistent that he have an active faith life and seek sanctification. While he spoke of his faith, he had not received sanctification. When he returned to New York to marry her, she felt torn. She loved him deeply, yet he did not express that sanctification that marked her own life so profoundly. But she could not wait any longer; she was unable to "resist his pleadings." So in the presence of a large number of friends and family, they married in the church. Two days later, they moved to Boston, where George worked. Despite leaving the family and the church she loved, she saw her marriage and moving to Boston as part of a "divine appointment."[65]

Foote found the move to Boston difficult. Her husband worked in Chelsea, a town about ten miles away. He could only visit Foote on the weekends. She was left alone in a new city with no family. The only thing that held her together was church. On her first Sunday in Boston, Foote marched to the local Methodist church, gave her membership letter to the minister, and offered testimony of her conversion and sanctification. The church, while not perfect, became Foote's primary social and spiritual home in her husband's absence.

At first, George Foote tolerated Julia's insistence on receiving sanctification. She understood sanctification as her primary identity marker and wanted others to experience the great love she had received, especially the person she loved most. However, he tired of her persistence and questioning. He told her, she writes, "[that if I] did not stop he would send me back home or to the crazy house." Foote tried to both reason with him and manage his anger. When she attempted to engage him in conversation, exasperated, he said, "Julia, I don't think I can ever believe myself as holy as you think you are." Foote urged him to believe in the power of complete sanctification and asked him to pray with her. As they prayed together, Foote felt something special: "There was an indescribable something between us something dark and high." This led her to recall the hymn from the British hymnist William Cowper, written one hundred years earlier: "God moves in a mysterious way, his wonders to perform." Later in that hymn, which she does not include, Cowper writes, "Behind a smiling providence, he hides a smiling face."[66] Foote perhaps also recalled those words as she knelt in prayer with her husband, letting him take the lead, despite the fact that she was sanctified (and thus more spiritually equipped than him).

Foote felt so close to George in that moment, a feeling that she would never regain. After that time in prayer, she "never beheld [her] husband's face clear and distinct, as before." A "dark shadow" clouded their marriage, causing her anxiety and stress. Not long after that moment, he was offered a job aboard a ship for six months that would leave her alone in Boston, collecting half his wages. Reluctantly, she agreed, realizing they could never bridge their differences. She also understood she could live out her sanctified life without her husband's resistance. She found herself torn—she strongly disapproved of her husband's departure, yet knew God called her to wait for him to return with "Christian forbearance and patient love." In the struggle between missing her husband and wanting to follow God, she sought solace in Isaiah 54, where the prophet Isaiah addressed a woman who could not have children. In Isaiah 54:5, the prophet proclaims, "For thy Maker is thine husband."[67] Foote meditated on this verse in her prayer closet when her husband left, trusting God while grieving.[68] In that moment, her God replaced the companionship of her husband.

Julia Foote's marriage to her husband, George, lasted several years in this long-distance format, with him coming home after six months or a year away only to leave again. While abroad, George struggled to practice his faith, as those around him were indifferent to religion. He told Julia that the captain approached him while he was praying, called him a "fool," and told him to get to work. Despite the difficulty, George chose to return to the ship. The subsequent separations were easier for Foote than the first, for God "saved [her] from a painful feeling at parting."[69] She could freely embrace sanctification and church life without the interference of her husband.

While Foote's husband did not understand or fully accept the nature of her calling, the spouses still mutually supported each other. Julia celebrated his safe returns from abroad. He sent her a portion of his wages. When he was away, Foote immersed herself in ministry. Later in her *Sketch*, after she accepted her call as an itinerant minister, she writes that she had heard that her husband had died aboard the ship several months earlier. The news hit her, she writes, "so suddenly as to almost cause me to sink beneath the blow." She immediately returned to Boston to ascertain more about his death and get their affairs in order. She tells her audience, "None but the dear Lord knew what my feelings were. I dared not complain, and thus cast contempt on my blessed Saviour."[70] Based on the whole of Foote's narrative, she had mixed feelings over his death. On the one hand, she grieved the loss of a spouse she loved. On the other hand, her husband had misunderstood what she saw to be the most essential part of her: her sanctification. As she, through the Spirit, drew closer to the Word of God (bodying the Word), she realized this movement also moved her away from her husband.

A Mystical Vision

While in Boston, when her husband was away working, Foote took joy in church ministry, praying with people and telling them about God's salvation. She began to think God called her "to a definite work" of itinerant ministry. Yet she saw herself as unworthy—"weak and ignorant."[71] Her initial resistance was in line with some Old Testament figures like Moses, Jeremiah, and Isaiah, who expressed hesitancy and wonder before accepting their divine call.[72] She turned to prayer and, while praying, an angel came to her. The angel held out a scroll with the words "Thee have I chosen to preach my Gospel without delay." Then the angel suddenly disappeared. Foote, tormented by the vision, could not sleep or eat. She understood the gravity of the call and feared accepting it. Foote also struggled with the call theologically. She had, she writes, "always been opposed to the preaching of women, and had spoken against it, though, I acknowledge, without foundation." She also knew that women preachers faced considerably more difficulties than their male counterparts.[73] To accept the call was to believe the Bible could be interpreted differently than she originally thought. She had to let go of her embedded understandings so she could body the Word fully.

In the end, the Holy Spirit's call won against the biblical injunction against women preachers. After the intense wrestling, she told God she "would do anything or go anywhere" in ministry as long as God made her calling clear. Not an hour later, she worried she had made a mistake. After all, her marriage had strained under her and her husband's differing spiritual states. Itinerant preaching could mean her relationships with her friends and family may fracture. As she prayed over this decision one Sunday night, a "supernatural presence" led her by the hand under a tree. Under the tree, she saw "God the Father, the Son, and the Holy Spirit" along with many angels. God the Father asked her if she would go anywhere God would tell her to go. Then she was led into water that looked like silver, and her hand was given to Christ. As she describes it, he "led me into the water and stripped me of my clothing, which at once vanished from sight. Christ then appeared to wash me, the water feeling quite warm." After Christ had finished washing her, he led her to shore, and she was presented with a new robe that the Father put upon her. Suddenly, she felt like she had become an angel. Christ led her back under the tree, where the Holy Spirit picked some fruit and gave it to her. After she ate it, the Father told her she was now prepared to minister, and when she again protested, Christ wrote a message for her and placed it on her heart. When she "came to herself," she saw her friends, worried about her health. When she described to them what happened, they said the letter on her heart "was to be shown in [her] life."[74]

Foote's vision is ripe with biblical imagery. Within the larger autobiography, this vision serves specifically as a call and sanction of Foote's preaching. The imagery includes allusions to Zechariah 3, where Foote derives "a brand plucked from the burning." In Zechariah 3, an angel removes the high priest Joshua's dirty clothes, proclaims him clean of sin, and replaces his clothing with "festal apparel." This was similar to how Christ replaced Foote's clothes with a clean robe. Foote may have also thought about Revelation in her vision. In Revelation 22, the author describes a "pure river of water of life, clear as crystal."[75] The tree of life stood in the middle and "yielded her fruit every month," just as Foote was given fruit from the tree by the water to eat. Revelation 21 spoke of the new Jerusalem as the bride of Christ. In the vision, Foote's hand was "given to Christ" (akin to "being given one's hand in marriage"), and he washed her.

Foote's inclusion of her vision in her autobiography serves as a foretaste of her more public ministry. She bodies a plethora of biblical imageries from both the Old and New Testaments in this one vision: those from Zechariah 3 and Revelation, that of the bride of Christ, and even those from the call narratives of the Hebrew prophets. Her fears would prove true: people would attempt to thwart her ministry. Nonetheless, assured of her sanctification and God's commission, she accepted her call to body the Word in itinerant ministry.

Dred Scott Decision

After she accepted her call and received her vision, Julia Foote immediately faced opposition from church leaders. She understood her situation as akin to the Dred Scott Supreme Court decision. The *Dred Scott v. Sandford* (1857) Supreme Court case was adjudicated in 1857, twenty-two years before she published her autobiography.[76] Born as an enslaved person, Dred Scott moved from Virginia to St. Louis, Missouri, with his enslaver, Peter Blow, who then sold Scott to an army doctor named Emerson. Emerson transported Scott to the free states and territories in the upper Midwest. Scott married while living there before returning to St. Louis with his enslaver. After his enslaver died, Scott and his wife, Harriet, because they had been married and bore a child while in the free states, thought they should go free. When the Scotts were set to be transferred to another enslaver instead of receiving emancipation, they brought a lawsuit to court. It eventually landed in the Supreme Court, where the court sided with the enslaver.[77] Justice Roger Taney wrote the opinion and claimed in the opening remarks, "The doctrine of 1776, that all [white] men 'are created free and equal,' is universally accepted and made the basis of all our institutions . . . and . . . the . . . *status* of the dominant race, is thus defined and fixed for ever." Taney then depicted

Black people as historically inferior and subordinate, beginning from when colonizers first kidnapped and enslaved Black Africans: "They [enslaved Black people] had for more than a century before been regarded as beings of an inferior order, and altogether unfit to associate with the white race, either in social or political relations; and so far inferior, that they had no rights which the *white man was bound to respect* [my emphasis]; and that the [Black man] might justly and lawfully be reduced to slavery for his benefit."[78]

Foote and her audience were aware of Taney's words. Though slavery had technically been abolished after the Civil War, the mindset of white supremacy prevailed in all regions and laws in the United States.

After she accepted her call to ministry and received some resistance at her own church, Foote tried to preach at other Boston-area African Methodist Episcopal Zion churches. She faced opposition from a certain Mr. Beman, a district leader. When he encouraged churches to forbid her to preach, she instead preached out of her home. Mr. Beman, along with a committee, called her into a conference, asking her if she would abide by their disciplines. She responded, "Not if the discipline prohibits me from what God has bidden me do, I fear God more than man."[79] The next day, he informed her that they had excommunicated her because of her preaching. In the aftermath, she wrote a letter to the conference, stating that she only intended to preach the gospel, had no ill feelings toward the committee, and asked for a hearing and a written statement of their opinion. She remarks that her letter "was slightly noticed and then thrown under the table. . . . It was only the grievance of a woman, and there was no justice meted out to women in those days. Even ministers of Christ did not feel that women had any rights which *they were bound to respect* [my emphasis]."[80]

Here, Foote applies the subjugation of Black people in the Dred Scott decision to the actions of the African Methodist Episcopal (AME) Zion conference. Foote's use of rhetoric is purposeful, to invoke "astonishment" by comparing the injustice of the decision with the rules of the church. The leaders would have recognized that rhetoric, having felt the decision's devastation two decades prior. By utilizing this rhetoric, Foote bodies a Word meant to subjugate Black people and uses it to demonstrate the hypocrisy of the church. The language of the decision indicts the church and its authorities. While the church advocated for abolition and equality for Black men, they did not do the same for Black women. Further, by invoking the Dred Scott verdict, Foote understands her struggle to preach and minister as a struggle that she did not face alone but would be faced by other Black women who hoped to preach.[81] In taking the church to task, she affirms herself as called by God to preach the gospel. She shows that this church, which was founded in resistance to the white church, oppresses women in the same manner that the white churches oppress Black people.

"Women and the Gospel"

In light of her experience with Mr. Beman and other church leaders, Foote takes the time to demonstrate her extensive knowledge of Scripture to defend her calling as an itinerant minister. After the Beman incident, she writes a chapter called "Women and the Gospel," where she outlines her case for preaching. She explains to her audience that "every man's hand is against us." She then engages in biblical exegesis to explain her rationale for women's preaching. She cites the Pentecost event recorded in Acts 2, including the verses Peter quotes from the book of Joel, which say women will prophesy. Women's preaching was not a temporary or onetime event, for in Pentecost, "women and men were classed together" in preaching the gospel. For Foote, Pentecost and the doctrine of holiness or sanctification go hand and hand. If women had lost the gift of prophecy or preaching after Pentecost, then men would have lost it as well.[82]

Foote references critics who said that if women receive a call to preach, they should be able to prove their credentials. Foote dryly suggests these "brethren" (male pastors) should have to prove the same credentials as those they require from women. Further, when Paul encourages others to help the women who collaborated with him, the women "did more than pour tea." In addition, Foote writes of early Christian women who went to heaven "happy and glorious in martyrdom. How nobly, how heroically, too, in later ages, have women suffered persecution and death for the name of the Lord Jesus." She compares herself to the women in the New Testament and the early church who preached and ministered, concluding, "I could see no miracle wrought for these women more than myself."[83] Here, she not only places herself as a liberative interpreter of Scripture, and in line with the Holy Spirit, but also likens herself to a character on equal standing to characters in Scripture.

As a preacher who speaks the Word and as a character in the continuing story of Scripture, Julia Foote, in her bodied self, resists the male centrism of her contemporaries' interpretation of the text, which understands Jesus's maleness as a qualifier for preaching. By invoking the history of women martyrs, Foote shows her confidence that the Christian faith, and its interpretation, has a history of resisting male-centric interpretations, even if its history is often a hidden one.

"Word to My Christian Sisters": A Holy Yes to Preaching

Foote not only argues for a justification of women preaching but speaks to women directly, providing them with encouragement and hope. Toward the end of her autobiography, Foote addresses "A Word to My Christian Sisters." In this chapter, she expresses how her words fail to describe the ecstasy of her calling: "I would that I could tell you a hundredth part of what God has revealed to me of his glory, especially on that never-to-be-forgotten night when I received my high and holy calling." The calling is different from her sanctification and more like a calling to ministry. She heard an otherworldly music like that "which Job, David and Isaiah speak of hearing at night upon their beds, or the one of which the Revelator says 'no man could learn.'" Then she asks her audience, "Sisters, shall not you and I unite with the heavenly host in the grand chorus?" While not admitting it directly, she puts herself on an almost equal plane as the Old Testament figures, claiming to hear something only they could hear. In so doing, she images herself as holy. Because she (and her women audience) are holy, hearing what only biblical characters could hear, they must ignore the voices of men who want to deny their calling: "[Do] not let what man may say or do, keep you from doing the will of the Lord or using the gifts you have for the good of others."

While Foote may have been using the term *man* to apply to all humanity, it applies explicitly to *men* given her next words: "Be not kept in bondage by those who say, 'We suffer not a woman to teach,' thus quoting Paul's words, but not rightly applying them."[84] This was from 1 Timothy 2, what most scholars now understand as a deutero-Pauline letter—that is, a letter not written by the apostle Paul himself but using his name as a pseudonym. Foote makes a case for women's preaching earlier in her narrative, quoting Joel 2 and Paul's calling of Priscilla to labor in the gospel in Romans 16:3 and citing the examples of the early women martyrs. She implies that the injunction against women's preaching is like the "deep waters" that they must pass through, with the anchor of God's calling to hold them "sure and steadfast." For Foote, disobedience in ignoring God's call upon her life seems graver than Paul's injunction against women's preaching. This "Word to My Christian Sisters" empowers women to trust the Word indwelling their bodies as they preach.

A Holy No: Refusal to Accommodate White Demands

After accepting her call to preach and facing resistance from Mr. Beman and other church leaders, Foote began her itinerant ministry. Foote, in her bodiment of the Word, deliberately defies societal expectations as she journeys as an itinerant evangelist. She bodies the liberative Word of God in resisting anyone who treats her as less than the image of God. With her body, she rejects a white supremacist view that only saw her in a servitude position. She acts in a way contrary to white societal expectations, and her bodily presence reminded white people they were not as powerful nor as superior as they thought they were.[85] In short, she goes against unwritten rules that most of society knew, but few would say out loud.

On one occasion, while traveling aboard a riverboat on the Erie Canal, she retired to the ladies' cabin to sleep, finding it completely empty. A white man, who discovered the men's cabins full, went to sleep in the ladies' cabin and found Foote already asleep. He demanded she get up and sleep elsewhere, claiming, "That n***** has no business here. My family are coming on board the boat at Utica, and they shall not come where a n***** is."[86] This man did not consider her "a lady" because of her skin color. She pretended to be asleep, not hearing him, hoping he would go away. She laid still, not moving, refusing to move even when the captain demanded she get up. She explains that she thought "it best not to leave the bed except by force."[87] In this instance, her refusal to move served as an act of resistance and affirmation. Foote's staying disrupts, if for but a night, the white world, establishing herself as a sacramental representation of Christ in the moment. Foote's refusal to move showed the man that he was not as powerful as he thought and that what he understood as normal was cruel and wrong.

Not long after this encounter, Foote again faced resistance, but this time in her preaching. Recalling how the white Methodist Episcopal Church treated both Richard Allen and her parents, Foote committed that where she preached would have no limitations on gender and race. Having gained a reputation in her itinerant ministry, she now held the power to dictate the terms of her preaching venues. While in Chillicothe, Ohio, a few deacons from a white Baptist congregation asked Foote to preach. Knowing the pastor disagreed with women preaching, she refused the invitation, explaining to her audience that their pastor spoke against women's preaching. This pastor even spoke harshly against those deacons who made the request. She mentions that the congregation eventually "dismissed him," presumably over his views. Foote includes this event in her autobiography because she wants to show the longevity of her ministry compared to the minister who forbade her to preach.[88] Her ministry outlasted that of the Baptist preacher.

She also refused to preach to a congregation that wanted to put boundaries on how Black people could participate. A white Methodist congregation in Ohio asked her to preach on the condition that Black people could not attend the service. She declined the invitation, claiming, "I would not agree to any such arrangement." She labels that church antigospel, claiming, "Prejudice had closed the door of their sanctuary against the [Black] people of the place, virtually saying 'the Gospel shall not be free to all.'" God called her to preach the gospel to *all* people and would not settle for limitations on who could listen. Later, while in Zanesville, Ohio, she encountered a white Methodist church that "opened their congregation" to Black people for the first time when Foote demanded it. In this instance, "hundreds were turned away," as the crowd was too large for the sanctuary. She explains that "God the Holy Ghost was powerfully manifest" in that meeting.[89]

As Foote reflects on her refusal to preach without barriers on who could listen, she quotes Scripture to back up her point. She cites Mark 16:15, where Jesus commands the disciples to preach the gospel "to every creature."[90] The churches that set limitations on her preaching implied that "the gospel shall not be free to all." However, she asserts, "Our benign Master and Saviour said: 'Go, preach my Gospel to all.'"[91] Foote bodies the Word in showing that these churches overtly disobey Scripture in denying Black people equal treatment with white people and in denying her authority as a Black woman preacher called by God. By describing Jesus as "benign," she implies that his demand is simple and innocuous, further exposing white supremacy's evil. Foote dislocates the comfortability of whiteness by not playing by its rules or limitations. Her refusal to acquiesce to white demands is akin to bodying the Word of freedom and, in so doing, exposing injustice for what it is.[92]

Threshing Sermon: Proof of the Holy Yes

After her refusal to set limitations on her preaching, Foote includes her sermonic material from that itinerant journey. As Lisa Zimerelli suggests, these sermons are "the earliest published sermons—as yet discovered—by an

African-American woman."[93] Through her sermons, Foote shows what happens when women say yes to God's calling to preach. In a particular instance, while traveling from Ohio to Detroit, Foote encountered a man who asked her to preach on Micah 4:13: "Arise and thresh, O daughter Zion, for I will make your horn iron and your hoofs bronze; you shall beat in pieces many peoples, and shall devote their gain to the Lord, their wealth to the Lord of the whole earth." Foote sees this sermon, and his question, as so important that she records the sermon in its entirety for her readers. First, she explains how she understood the people in the biblical era to thresh—that is to separate the seed from the plant—by having animals stomp upon it. Of course, she interjects, this would be different from how her audience would have threshed corn. Foote remarks that the passage could in one sense apply to "preachers of the Word." Preachers must help the people excise (thresh) the sin from their lives, so they could seek God fully. However, she explains, it also "has a direct reference to all God's people, who were and are commanded to arise and thresh."[94] She connects the universal call to thresh—to gain souls for Christ—with Joel 2:28–29:

> *Then afterward*
> *I will pour out my spirit on all flesh;*
> *your sons and your daughters shall prophesy,*
> *your old men shall dream dreams,*
> *and your young men shall see visions.*
> *Even on the male and female slaves,*
> *in those days, I will pour out my spirit.*

For Foote, the universal call to Christ could only be accomplished when *all* people: men and women, young and old, Black and white, could proclaim the gospel.

She further ponders the role of the threshing instrument and likened it to the gospel's sharp presence. Just as the flail or the hoof separates the wheat from the plant, so does the "Gospel flail" thresh Satan out of sinners.[95] This "Gospel flail" could also be known as the "sword of the Spirit," a reference to Ephesians 6:17. The sword of the Spirit / gospel flail worked to convict people of their sins and cause them to turn toward God. Foote remarks that after preaching that sermon, the person who originally asked her to preach it was converted. She praises God for his salvation and then addresses her audience to act on her words: "Reader, have you this salvation an ever-flowing fountain in your soul?" before ending the chapter.[96] When women like Foote were freely able to say yes to God's calling them to preach, God converted the hardest of hearts. By including her sermon in her autobiography, Foote provides evidence that women could successfully preach, and that their sermons effectively shared the gospel. She bodies the words of Scripture to point to the Word of salvation, the "ever-flowing fountain."

A Holy Yes: Come and Be Holy

Foote wraps up her *Sketch* like any good preacher would, with a call to not only Christ but faith and sanctification: "Why not yield, believe, and be sanctified now, while reading?" She hopes the book achieved its purpose of promoting "the cause of holiness in the church."[97]

Before this ending, she outlines in detail her concept of holiness, and why she believed it is essential to faith. Foote's penultimate chapter, "Love Not the World," focuses upon how a person of faith is not to be conformed to this world.[98] As she surveys Christians, she remarks that though they claimed the Christian identity, their witness betrayed them. She saw this when so-called Christians abused and criticized her based on her gender and race. She also specifically addresses ministers of the church, claiming that "many profess to teach, but few are able to feed the lambs." She exhorts leaders to live holy lives—while they cannot be perfect, they can work toward Christian perfection. Here, she cites John Wesley in her depiction of Christian perfection, also known as holiness: "an extinction of every temper contrary to love."[99] This is what it meant to be holy—to live a loving life toward everyone. This love aligns with the bodying of the Word—to have the Word live inside her meant to love as Christ loved.

Conclusion: A Style that Defines Imagination

For Foote, bodying the Word means using a variety of words to say yes to things that align with God's reign and no to any injustice. The words she uses came from Scripture, current events around her, and teachings from her theological heritage. The way she bodies the words expands an understanding of Word, incarnation, and bodies. Foote's rhetorical proficiency disrupts traditional understandings of the Word and who can preach it. She models the distinction between "the power of Scripture" and the "power of empire" that had a hand in writing Scripture.[100] In Foote's context of the nineteenth-century United States, white male power and the written word—including Scripture—were wedded together. Foote, by writing her own autobiography and including her sermons, disrupts this alignment. As she bodies the Word, she exposed that words always connect with bodies. The written word concretely affects bodies, such as in Dred Scott's case. In addition, bodies go beyond those who write words.

Rather than words "being set in stone," Foote's appropriation of the stylistic devices of Scripture and contemporary political documents shows that words can flex and adapt. Words can be applied in new ways to new contexts and hold new meanings. As such, Scripture is not limited to a singular meaning. Rather, Foote's context becomes the backdrop where she theologized and analyzed the Word of God. Her bodying of the Word resists interpretations that apply the Word's presence only to particular bodies. The Word becoming flesh does not mean words become solidified in the patriarchal realm. The Word becomes enfleshed in Foote herself as she preaches. Her work in engaging both Scripture and contemporary documents points to the fissures and messiness inherent with the incarnation. Further, in her engagement not just with Scripture but various texts, she demonstrates and expands a notion of the divine that is present, but not confined, in the Bible. For Foote, bodying the Word means that she can deploy a multiplicity of texts for demonstrating how the divine works through her. Thus, at the end of her *Sketch*, she can praise and share the good news of the one who "is able to do exceeding abundantly . . . according to the power that worketh" within her.[101]

4

Sojourner Truth
The Spirit's Withness

How strange are the events of our lives. How little
we know of the world we live in, especially of the
spiritual world by which we are surrounded. . . .
I did not think you were laying the foundation
of such an almost world-wide reputation when I
wrote that little book for you, but I rejoice and am
proud that you can make your power felt with so
little book education.[1]

Olive Gilbert, Sojourner Truth's first biographer, wrote
this letter in 1870, twenty years after she first drafted
Truth's autobiography in 1850. In 1843, Sojourner Truth
had just changed her name from Isabella Van Wagenen,

shunning any outside conventions that would define her and naming herself in light of her divine vision. Since that 1850 edition, several other biographers in the twentieth and twenty-first centuries have written about Sojourner Truth at length, working to tell the story of her life and dispel common misconceptions about her and her ministry.[2] Sojourner Truth's works and words also function theologically. Her works and words depict a Holy Spirit present *within* her. Concurrently, she understood the Holy Spirit authorizing her to bear witness. With the power of the Holy Spirit, she bears witness as divinely called in a world that considered her less than human. Her words also testified to a Holy Spirit as *withness*, including both the meaning of the Spirit within and the notion of bearing witness.[3] To be with someone is to bear witness, and to bear witness is to be with another—whether that another is a human person or, in Truth's case, the Holy Spirit. The Holy Spirit as withness allows her to celebrate her Black body throughout her life, despite the numerous struggles she faced.

Beginnings: An Afro-Dutch Mysticism

Sojourner Truth was born about 1797 in Ulster County, New York, one hundred miles north of New York City.[4] Her mother, Mau Mau Bett (formal name Elizabeth), gave her the name Isabella, which some people shortened to "Bell."[5] Isabella was the second youngest of about ten children. At the time of her birth, her older siblings had all been separated and sold by their enslaver. As a child, her mother and father, Bomefree (meaning "tree" in Dutch), told her stories about her siblings, grieving their absence and wanting the young Isabella to know of her family.[6]

Isabella's mother was her first spiritual teacher. Mau Mau Bett incorporated some elements of African cosmology into her spirituality, which Truth later wove into her own withness. Isabella's maternal grandmother was from Africa, most likely from the west central region of Africa—the Kongo region.[7] Her mother weaved her African heritage with the Dutch culture of her enslavers, paving a way for Isabella to establish her "most curious and original views."[8] At night, after Mau Mau Bett's duties had ended, she told Isabella and her younger sibling about God: "My children, there is a God, who hears and sees you. . . . He lives in the sky,' . . . and when you are beaten, or cruelly treated, or fall into any trouble, you must ask help of him, and he will always hear and help you." The God who lived in the sky was also a comfort for her siblings, whom enslavement had separated. Mau Mau Bett, pointing at the sky, told Isabella, "Those are the same stars, and that is the same moon, that look down upon your brothers and sisters, and which they see as they look up to them, though they are ever so far away from us, and each other."[9] Mau Mau Bett's teachings about God enabled Isabella to know the divine was with her, bearing withness, and loved her as she suffered at the hands of white supremacy.

In addition to her mother's teachings, Isabella's theology was formed in part through holidays and rituals, such as Pinkster. Pinkster was the Dutch name for Pentecost. In the Bible, Pentecost was when the Holy Spirit descended upon the disciples in Acts 2 after Jesus's ascension into heaven. Pinkster helped Isabella understand the freedom and equality that accompanied the Spirit's withness.

Any interpretation of Pinkster in the United States is "speculative" because of lack of familiarity with resources and lack of firsthand accounts in Dutch.[10] The few accounts that still exist are in English, written from an outsider's perspective. Black and white—enslaved, enslaver, and freed persons—all celebrated the Pinkster holiday, which lasted for a few days. Black people enslaved by the Dutch who lived in New York became familiar with Pinkster and brought their own rituals and traditions to it. Some historians theorize that the emotional content of Pentecost—the immediate indwelling of the Holy Spirit—bore resemblance to some African traditions and rituals. In New York, it became a uniquely Black American holiday.[11]

Not only was Pinkster a religious holiday, but it also served as a place to build community among enslaved Black people who often felt isolated and without a support system. In Dutch New York, enslaved people did not live alongside many other enslaved persons and often resided in rural settings. The holiday enabled them the time and space to come together. They were able to cease work for a few days and enjoy one another's company. Pinkster blended both Dutch Reformed culture and African rituals to produce a celebratory atmosphere enabling "African Americans to maintain and reinforce African folkways, and to claim cultural space for themselves in an oppressive system."[12] In her teachings, Mau Mau Bett passed on elements of Pinkster to the young Isabella, including its Christian and African roots. Black people who would not have access to baptism or the rites of the church "could experience regeneration and salvation without sacraments or church membership" at Pinkster.[13] Isabella enthusiastically participated: "As a Pinkster reveler, [Isabella] engaged in European folk dancing as well as rhythmic, muscular, erotic African performances."[14] These erotic dances enabled her to love her own body and also reminded her of the Holy Spirit who dwells with and in all bodies, Black and white, enslaved and freed.

While Pinkster held spiritual significance, it also contained a carnivalesque atmosphere—including drunkenness, dancing, and revelry.[15] One historian describes how Pinkster "meant so much to Sojourner Truth that one year she resolved to go even if it meant returning to her former master, an abusive man who had sold her five-year-old son illegally and from whom she had fled."[16] Indeed, later in life, after Isabella walked away from her enslaver, she "'looked back into Egypt,' and everything looked 'so pleasant there,' as she saw retrospectively all her former companions enjoying their freedom for at least a little space, as well as their wonted convivialities, and in her heart she longed to be with them."[17] While she was enslaved, Pinkster, even if for a few days, reminded her of the joy and pleasure that could be found in freedom, the freedom to be with her people. Pinkster revealed to Isabella that the Spirit's withness was one of freedom.

While Isabella would ultimately downplay Pinkster in favor of the Methodist holiness movement of the first half of the nineteenth century, the bodied element it contained, including the affirmation of Blackness and Black bodies, followed her throughout her life. She held on to the celebration and temporary freedom that coincided with

Pinkster, even as she rejected the drinking, dancing, and revelry it so often held.

In Every Trial: Growing Up in Enslavement

At nine years old, her Dutch enslaver separated her from her parents by selling her to another family, the Nealys, who could only speak and understand English. She recalled that in "this sale she was connected with a lot of sheep." Up to that point, young Isabella had only spoken Dutch. Her enslavers could not communicate with her, and as a result, they would beat her. She received the worst beating of her life while with the Nealys. In that moment, "she did not forget the instructions of her mother, to go to God in all her trials, and every affliction." Still a girl, she thought that God could only hear her if she spoke audibly. She pleaded with God aloud, asking God "if He thought it was right" that her enslaver should beat her.[18] Absent from her supportive family, she saw God's presence with her when her enslaver tortured her. She also was not afraid to question God, asking God why this would happen to her. At times, when the opportunity arose, she fled to a private place where she could turn to God in her sorrows. Though Isabella could sense God's presence, she could not understand her unjust suffering, questioning if God really was *with* her. Several months into the arrangement, her father came to visit her. While they were out of earshot of her enslavers, she explained her difficulties and asked if he might help her find a new enslaver who treated her more humanely. He told her he would do his best. After that conversation, Isabella would walk to their conversation spot and pray over and over that God would deliver her from the cruel Nealys. She hoped in both her father and God for deliverance. Eventually, her father's promise would come to fruition, and not long afterward, she was sold to a fisherman and tavern owner. About eighteen months later, the now teenaged Isabella was sold to John Dumont, with whom she remained for eighteen years.

Now living with the Dumonts, Isabella had fully learned how to speak and understand English. Never knowing a different form of life, Isabella began to internalize the enslaver's religion. She confessed her shortcomings to her enslaver. As a teenager and young adult woman, she "looked upon her master as a God; and believed that he knew of and could see her at all times, even as God himself." Reflecting upon her mindset at that point, Sojourner Truth looked back "at the absurdity of the claims so arrogantly set up by the masters, over beings designed by God to be as free as kings."[19] Coming into her own as a young adult woman, Isabella had to process her status as an enslaved woman alongside the teachings of her mother and her experiences of Pinkster. She knew God was always present, that God heard her in her trouble, but, simultaneously, had been conditioned to obey enslavers at the expense of her own well-being. In a sense, she faced two competing religions: that of her mother and that of her enslaver.

In time, Isabella fell in love with another enslaved man from a neighboring area, Robert. He would covertly come to visit her. When his enslavers found out, they beat him harshly and demanded he take a wife who had the same enslaver. Robert and Isabella never saw each other again. Isabella, in turn, was partnered with another enslaved man,

Thomas, and gave birth to five children. She held complicated feelings over her status as a mother and wife. In many ways, she was forced to marry (though the marriage was not legal according to law) and bear children to perpetuate the property of her enslaver. The endless work and forced mothering contradicted the God whom she believed heard her cries of injustice. She wondered if God was really *with* her.

Walking Away: An Inward Nudging

Throughout her *Narrative*, Truth described premonitions, or inward nudgings, that can be identified with the Holy Spirit. This inward sense, voice, or feeling helped her discern what to do. The notion of inner nudging, or an inner voice, correlates to the apostle Paul's description of the Spirit: the "Spirit intercedes with sighs too deep for words."[20] She saw the Spirit as present within her, directing her where to go. Truth's walking away from her enslaver demonstrates such inward nudging, which allows for boldness. Isabella was supposed to have received free papers on July 4, 1827. However, her enslaver, John Dumont, demanded she stay. In the previous year, she suffered a hand injury, which Dumont claimed limited her productivity. Isabella, frustrated at his decision, began crafting her escape. She would escape after she had accomplished the task of spinning one hundred pounds of sheep's wool, and as she spun the wool, she began to plot her escape. She conversed with God, asking how she should do it, as she was afraid to leave at night. After some time, she had an idea: "She could leave just before the day dawned, and get out of the neighborhood where she was known before the people were much astir. 'Yes,' said she, fervently, 'that's a good thought! Thank you, God, for that thought!'"[21] The Holy Spirit within her had inspired her to figure out the details on how to escape her enslaver.

In the morning, before the sun rose, she carried her baby, Sophia, in one arm and her belongings in the other and walked out of her enslaver's house. After walking far enough away to be out of their eyesight, Truth was unsure as to what to do next. She sat down, fed her baby, and prayed to God "to direct her to some safe asylum."[22] Knowing that the Quakers opposed slavery, she headed toward their settlement, where she encountered a Levi Rowe. Though on his deathbed, he directed her to Isaac Van Wagenen, who was known for helping enslaved people.[23]

Upon arrival at the Van Wagenens, they gladly gave her a job and a place to stay. She did not enjoy peace for long. Soon, her enslaver, Dumont, found her staying with the Van Wagenens. He said, "Well, Bell, so you've run away from me." She retorted, "No, I did not run away; I walked away by day-light." She reminded him that *he* had broken his promise of freeing her at the agreed-upon time. His only response was "You must go back with me." Again, she emphasized, "No, I won't go back with you." He then demanded that if she wouldn't return with him, he should at least take her baby. She again shot him down. After that, Isaac Van Wagenen intervened. He told Dumont that while he didn't believe in slavery, he would purchase Isabella and her baby's freedom if Dumont would leave them alone. Dumont agreed. As Dumont was preparing to leave, Isaac Van Wagenen, within earshot of Dumont, told Isabella to not call him master, for "there is but one master; and he who is your master is my master."[24] Isabella was bound to no one but God.

"Oh God, I Did Not Know You Were So Big!": Isabella's Conversion

While Isabella basked in her freedom, she still was disentangling the religion she had received from her enslavers from the spirituality she had inherited from her parents. After walking away from her enslaver, Mr. Dumont, she decided to return to him. She missed celebrating Pinkster (Pentecost) and seeing her family and friends. She felt a premonition that Dumont would visit her and told the Van Wagenens her inclinations. When they asked her why she felt that way, she replied that it was a feeling within her. Her instinct was correct, as Mr. Dumont came to the Van Wagenen household. She informed him of her intention to leave with him, inwardly fueled by the desire to celebrate Pinkster, and readied herself and her baby to leave.

As Isabella approached his carriage, she stopped in her tracks. She exclaimed that "God revealed himself to her . . . with all the suddenness of a flash of lightning, showing her 'in the twinkling of an eye, that he was all over'—that he pervaded the universe—'and that there was no place where God was not.'" She felt a conviction of her sin within her for forgetting God's presence "as ever-present help in time of trouble." Visioning inwardly, she sensed a great fear in encountering the divine presence so intimately, "as if [God] had been a being like herself; and she would now fain have hid herself in the bowels of the earth, to have escaped

[God's] dread presence." Whether or not Isabella was consciously aware of this phrasing, the fear of seeing and being seen by the divine presence echoes Old Testament figures like Moses, who, in encountering the burning bush, hides his face from God in fear. By deploying biblical language in her encounter with the divine, Isabella imagined herself as a prophet, specially called by God.

She came out of her vision and to the present moment, finding Dumont had left. But this powerful moment made her ponder inwardly what had just occurred. "Oh God, I did not know you were so big," she uttered. She struggled to make sense of what had happened to her: "'Who are you?' she exclaimed, as the vision brightened into a form distinct, beaming with the beauty of holiness, and radiant with love. She then said, audibly addressing the mysterious visitant—'I know you, and I don't know you.' Meaning, 'You seem perfectly familiar; I feel that you not only love me, but that you always have loved me—yet I know you not—I cannot call you by name.'"[25]

After some wrestling within her soul, "with the intensity of this desire, till breath and strength seemed failing," she said, "It is Jesus." Coming to a new awareness, she was in awe of "the union existing between herself and Jesus—Jesus, the transcendently lovely as well as great and powerful . . . and she watched for his bodily appearance, and when he came, she would go and dwell with him, as with a dear friend."

Truth's mystical vision of the divine, initiated by the "flash of lightning," demonstrates her desire for God as deification. If deification is understood as God becoming human (incarnate) so humans can become God (deified) through the work of the Spirit, it becomes possible to intuit the role of pneumatology in Truth even where she does not explicitly mention the Spirit. The Spirit's indwelling, symbolized by the lightning strike, also allowed her to envision Jesus. The Spirit within her enabled her to witness that God is everywhere—"there is no place, not even in hell, where [God] is not."[26] This echoes Psalm 139, where the psalmist describes that God knows them intimately, and because of that, they praise God because, they write, "I am fearfully and wonderfully made." That Truth implied in the visitation to the divine presence "that you [God] have always loved me" correlates with the psalmist's declaration that God knew them and loved them, even before they were born. God loved her Black female body. In this moment, she received love and joy from the divine invitation, whom she named Jesus. In the visitation, she realized that just as she desired God, God also desired her.

The Spirit within Isabella, who came to her like a flash of lightning and enabled her to withness the divine presence, was with her as she named the presence "Jesus." The union between her and Jesus was also initiated by the Spirit within her, even though she did not mention the Spirit's presence concretely. The vision, combined with her references to Scripture, demonstrates that Isabella saw "the continual action of God upon the soul" in such a way that allowed her to partake in the divine nature—to become godified by the Holy Spirit. Mystically, she understood (through the work of the Holy Spirit) that the divine presence had always been with her, even when she could not name it. After this moment, she would no longer want to go back to a life of enslavement. She had found freedom in the Spirit's withness, who knew her intimately and had always loved her.

Inward Nudging: Finding Her Son Peter

Securing her own freedom enabled Isabella to fight for her son's. While she was still enslaved by Dumont, he had sold her five-year-old son Peter, who, after being sold again, was taken south to Alabama. According to New York law at the time, selling enslaved persons outside of New York was illegal, as the state was beginning to implement laws to free enslaved persons when they were twenty-one. Isabella, because she had walked to freedom, was unaware of Peter ending up in Alabama. Once informed, she went directly back to her enslaver, demanding the return of her child. Her enslaver, Mrs. Dumont, scoffed, "How can you get him? And what have you to support him with, if you could? Have you any money?" Isabella responded, testifying to the Spirit's withness within her: "'No,' answered Bell, 'I have no money, but God has enough, or what's better! And I'll have my child again.' These words were pronounced in the most slow, solemn, and determined measure and manner."[27]

In that moment of retelling the story, her amanuensis Olive Gilbert observed, "And in speaking of it, she says, 'Oh my God! I know I'd have him agin. I was sure God would help me to get him. Why, I felt so tall within—I felt as if the power of a nation was with me!' The impressions made by Isabella on her auditors, when moved by lofty or deep feeling, can never be transmitted to paper."[28] Gilbert perceived that Truth's determination was not just in her mind but felt bodily.

Truth's assurance that she would see her son again, marked by the Spirit's assurance within her, sustained her determination. Someone told her to seek help from some Quakers, who listened to her story and provided her with lodging. They brought her to Kingston, New York, where they directed her to go to the grand jury. Thinking the grand jury was a singular person, she walked up to anyone she saw and explained her loss of Peter. After being mocked by more than one person, she finally found the grand jury, who, after asking her to swear upon a book, which she thought must be the Bible, gave her a warrant to give to the constable for the return of her son. Unfortunately, the constable served the warrant to the wrong person, and Peter's enslaver escaped. Finally, with the assistance of a stranger, she found a lawyer who agreed to help her. The lawyer told her that because the enslaver had broken the law by taking Peter out of state, he could be sued and imprisoned. Peter's enslaver, fearing punishment, brought Peter back to New York. The lawyer eventually secured Peter's return, arranging for them to meet and she to confirm that he was indeed her son. At first, Peter, conditioned by his enslaver, was afraid of his mother, having not seen her for several years. Finally, he recognized her. Embracing him, Isabella traced her hands along the scars on his face and back that he had suffered while under the enslaver's wrath.[29] Isabella, who had prayed daily for his return, finally had him in her arms.

The inner voice—the Holy Spirit—allowed Isabella to function as witness to her son's rescue. The Spirit in her gave her assurance she would find her son—such assurance that she felt as if she had "the power of a nation" within her.[30] The Spirit's presence was also *with* her as her heart was *with* her son. She had prayed daily for his return, begging Jesus to plead to God on her behalf.[31] Gilbert describes how Isabella's bodily deep desire for her son could "never be transmitted to paper . . . till by some Daguerrian act, we are enabled to transfer the look, the gesture, the tones of voice, . . . and the spirit-stirring animation that . . . pervades all she says."[32] Isabella did not accept no, despite being unable to read or write or secure money—all things that would help her procure her son. In touch with the Spirit within her, knowing herself as divinely inspired, she continued to search, seek, and find him, refusing to give up. In her quest for her son, she bore withness to the God who saw her, and the God who would and did deliver her son to her.

New York City: Testing the Spirits

After Isabella secured Peter's freedom, she felt she needed to leave Kingston and pursue opportunities for both of them in New York City. She left for New York and resided with a James LaTourette, "a wealthy merchant, and a Methodist in religion," though, in the religious upheaval of the mid-nineteenth century, he had outgrown organized religion and held instead meetings in his own home.[33] Having joined a Methodist church while in Kingston and fighting for Peter's return, she transferred her membership to Zion Church in New York City, an African American Methodist church where she could worship fully and freely. When her sister Sophia came to visit her, she told Isabella that they had a brother also living in the city and introduced Isabella to her brother Michael. Michael told Isabella and Sophia that their sister Diana, who had died months earlier, had also attended Isabella's church. Because their enslaver sold Diana before Isabella was born, Isabella had never met her older sister. When Michael described Diana's features, Isabella instantly recognized her. She had worshipped alongside Diana at Zion Church! She described how Diana was "with whom she had knelt at the altar, and with whom she had exchanged the speaking pressure of the hand." Isabella thought to herself, "Was I not, at the time, struck with the peculiar feeling of her hand—the bony hardness so just like mine? And yet I could not know she was my sister; and now I see she looked so like my mother."[34] The three siblings cried over the death of Diana and the missed opportunity to be a family. They may have remembered their mother, who had encouraged them to look into the night sky and remember that their siblings, though scattered about, looked at that same moon and stars. The God who looked down on them as enslaved children surely was with them and bore witness to their pain and sorrow.

Unfortunately, Isabella's sorrows would not leave her. As her son Peter grew, he began to rebel against her, squandering the money given to him for school and getting into trouble. He bore both the emotional and physical scars of his trauma while enslaved and found friendship and community in the streets of New York. Isabella, more than once, had to bail him out of bad situations and even jail. Finally, after one instance when he was arrested and Isabella refused to help him, he called upon a respected Black barber named Peter Williams. Williams bailed the young Peter out of jail on condition that he become a sailor on a whaling ship. The young Peter promised to do so, telling his mother, Isabella, of the plan. The week after he had left, Isabella still harbored doubt regarding Peter's whereabouts, expecting to hear about him from a friend or see him on the street. After several months passed, she received some letters from him, proving that he was on a ship, asking about his sisters and family. She last received a letter from him dated September 19, 1841, then never heard from him again. While the cause of his death was never recorded, he most likely died from the smallpox epidemic that raged through ships at that time.[35] Isabella would never know.

While struggling with parenting Peter and making ends meet, Isabella also found her time in New York one in which she explored, tested, and expanded her faith. While she learned and grew with the congregation at Zion, she also struggled to discern for herself what she believed. She constantly worked to make ends meet and attended Bible classes with both Black and white Methodists in the evening.[36] As part of her church involvement, she acted as a missionary to "the most wretched abodes of vice and misery," sometimes going where no middle class, churchgoing, white woman would, establishing prayer meetings. She also participated in other prayer meetings where people "would [become] delirious with excitement, and then exhausted from over-action." In one such meeting, people were shouting, stomping, and clapping so much that they knocked Isabella over, stomping upon her body and leaving bruises. She discerned that God had nothing to do with "such worship" and that the excitement was not from the Holy Spirit.[37] While she could testify to the Holy

Spirit's presence in "the most wretched abodes of vice," she could not attribute emotional expression and outburst alone to the Spirit's withness.

At one point in this spiritual exploration, Isabella found herself involved with a cult. After lodging with a Methodist family, Mr. Pierson, who supervised one of the ministries with which she was involved, asked her to live with him as a domestic servant. Pierson likened himself to the biblical character of Elijah, seeing it as his duty and vision to host meetings and explain his version of the kingdom of God. Pierson's devotional status led Robert Matthews to seek him out to form a spiritual community. Matthews called himself "Matthias," believed God told him to not shave his beard, and drew curious crowds with his street preaching. Matthias also claimed to be Jewish, preaching the kingdom of the Father, and not the Son. When Matthias and Pierson met, they both admitted "the direct influence of the Spirit, and the transmission of spirits from one body to another." At first, Isabella found Matthias's appearance, charisma, and unique interpretations compelling. She even offered to do Matthias's laundry at one of her multiple jobs. However, their later interpretations would contradict some of her closely held beliefs. Matthias and Pierson taught the subordination of women, believed they were Jewish and thus did not eat pork, denounced prayer as unimportant, and taught that when people died, their souls entered other bodies. They also encouraged Isabella and others in the commune to hold property in common, and by the time Isabella began to have doubts, she had already put her meager savings and belongings toward the benefit of the group.[38] Isabella—who had turned to God frequently in prayer, saw the Son Jesus as an intercessor for her, and believed the Holy Spirit was with and within her—found herself in a community she could not escape.

Thankfully, her time with Matthias's kingdom of the Father was not long. Eventually, Matthias and Pierson prepared to move away from the city to a farm where they could live out their beliefs, while Isabella stayed behind, finding a place to rent elsewhere. However, then Pierson died under mysterious circumstances. Matthias was arrested, tried, and declared not guilty of Pierson's murder, and one of the cult members accused Isabella of murdering him.[39] Isabella, left broke after putting her savings and possessions with the cult, found herself impoverished and disillusioned. She realized Matthias and Pierson had exploited her frugality to perpetuate their own wealth. Surveying her time in New York City, she realized she needed to change how she understood both herself and her surroundings. No longer would she trust what other people said about God or the Holy Spirit without question; rather, she would turn to the Spirit within her before discerning her next steps. The Spirit's withness would tell her what she needed to do.

Naming Herself: From Isabella to Sojourner

Isabella, trusting the Spirit's withness, decided to leave New York City and go east toward Long Island. She knew her friends and family would think her strange for leaving and so did not tell them. An hour before she departed, Isabella informed her landlord she was leaving and put a few articles of clothing in a pillowcase for the trip. In addition, she told her landlord that "her name was no longer

Isabella, but SOJOURNER; and that she was going east."[40] She went with a purpose, to "lecture"—that is, "exhorting the people to embrace Jesus, and refrain from sin, the nature and origin of which she [would explain] to them in accordance with her own most curious and original views." Truth felt an inner peace, knowing the Spirit was within her and guiding her, "her heart strong in the faith that her true work lay before her, and that the Lord was her director; and she doubted not he would provide for and protect her."[41] She avowed to follow the Spirit's lead and trust the Spirit within herself.

While traveling, Sojourner Truth attended Christian meetings of multiple denominations, where she had the opportunity to preach and lecture. As she gained notoriety, she began to organize her own lectures and events. Like Jesus's instructions in sending the disciples, Truth relied on the hospitality of strangers in finding shelter or a meal and took no extra provisions.[42] Also like Jesus, she found her strongest supporters among not the rich but the poor. In finding lodging, she remarked, "it was much easier to find an unoccupied corner in a small house than in a large one; and if a person possessed but a miserable roof over his head, you might be sure of a welcome to part of it."[43] Perhaps Truth had thought of Jesus's response to the rich young ruler in Luke 18:25: "It is easier for a camel to go through a needle's eye, than for a rich man to enter into the kingdom of God."[44] While Truth would later converse with the likes of Abraham Lincoln and Harriet Beecher Stowe, she never forgot the hospitality of those who shared their meager homes with her. She understood the Spirit's witness especially among and with the poor and oppressed.

A Resting Place: The Northampton Community

After traveling wherever she was invited—both in churches and in homes—and leading meetings herself, Sojourner Truth desired to find a place to call home for a season. She found that home with the Northampton Community in Massachusetts. Northampton was a commune that espoused abolition, integration, gender equality, and some millennial spirituality.[45] In Northampton, Truth soon became a leader. She captivated its members with her sermons, worked hard at her assigned tasks, and took care of the ill.[46] One community member described her this way: "[She was] a great favorite in our meetings, both on account of her remarkable gift in prayer, and still more remarkable talent for singing, . . . and the aptness and point of her remarks."[47] The commune recognized Truth bore the Spirit's withness in her sermons and leadership.

While in the commune, she had the space to learn, test out, and expand her views. This included her view of Scripture. Because she could not read, she first asked adults to read Scripture to her, but if she asked them to reread the passage, they would explain it rather than read the text. So she asked children to read the Bible to her, who did not question her if she asked them to reread passages and who did not offer their own explanations. This was so Truth could discern for herself what the text meant. As she listened to the Scriptures, "she wished to compare the teachings of the Bible with the witness within her; and she came to the conclusion, that the spirit of truth spoke in those records, but the recorders of those truths had intermingled with them ideas and suppositions of their own."

The divinizing Spirit who united Truth to God also affirmed her personhood and ability to interpret biblical texts. The Spirit within her contested passages in the Bible that Truth would deem to have less authority, based on their limitation of freedom. The "spirit within her" let her bear witness to the Scriptures, allowing her to determine the "recorders of those truths" had agendas of their own that needed fulfilling.

Truth's inner witness of the Spirit enabled her body (which included her mind) to become the site of the divine whereby she could discern the validity of the Scriptures. She realized while reading the creation account in Genesis that she should not interpret Scripture literally—otherwise, it would not make sense. For instance, because God was all powerful and was omnipresent, God did not need rest, or rest from caring for creation, as Genesis 2:2–3 infers. In addition, since God was not human, God did not need to walk in the "cool of the day" for exercise.[48] She loved Scripture, believed deeply that God is love, and took the Bible seriously, which meant she could not see it as inerrant. Rather, the Spirit within her enabled her to discern the character of God through the witness of Scripture. Her deepening understanding of Scripture was an effect of her sanctification or deification—or as John Wesley describes, "the continual action of God upon the soul."

The Demise of Northampton and
Her Ministry Post-Narrative

Those who knew Truth saw the Spirit's witness surrounding her, continually working in her life. One such person was Olive Gilbert, her first biographer, who visited the commune at Northampton. Gilbert was an activist and scholar whose inheritance and frugal living allowed her the time to devote to abolitionist causes. Because Truth could not write or read, she needed someone like Gilbert to convey her story. Truth published her *Narrative* when she was around fifty-three. Gilbert described Truth as having "her heart upon having a little home of her own, even at this late hour of life."[49] While many may have considered Truth to be in her later years when it was published, much of her activist work and preaching occurred after the *Narrative*.

At the time Gilbert wrote Truth's *Narrative*, the Northampton utopian community was slowly dissolving, spurred on by debt and the realization that they could not live out their full values.[50] Truth fell full force into itinerant ministry and lecturing, preaching and singing in churches, and advocating for abolition. With the help of William Lloyd Garrison, a prominent abolitionist, and the American Anti-Slavery Society, she could sell her *Narrative* as she lectured.[51]

At the close of the *Narrative*, Gilbert depicted Sojourner Truth's spirituality as robust, despite the heartbreak she incurred: "With all her fervor, and enthusiasm, and speculation, her religion is not tinctured in the least with gloom. No doubt, no hesitation, no despondency, spreads a cloud over her soul; but all is bright, clear, positive, and at times ecstatic. Her trust is in God, and from him she looks for good, and not evil. She feels that 'perfect love casteth out fear,'" a reference to 1 John 4:18.[52] Gilbert recognized the Holy Spirit as within Sojourner Truth and accompanying her in her ministry. Knowing God loved her gave her the strength to face frightening situations as she continued to preach and advocate for abolition, women's suffrage, and equality for all people.

"Arn't I a Woman"

Truth's understanding of the Spirit as witness became fully present in her "Arn't I a Woman" sermon, delivered in 1851 at a women's convention in Akron, Ohio.[53] The exact words of the sermon are debated; there is no direct transcript.[54] The earliest-recorded version, compiled by Marius Robinson for the *Anti-Slavery Bugle*, attempted to convey the meaning rather than provide a dictation. Twelve years after Truth delivered her sermon, Frances Gage, a woman's rights activist who was present at the meeting, wrote down what she could remember of Truth's sermon for the *New York Independent*. In doing so, she stereotyped Truth as a southern enslaved person on a plantation, "minstrelizing her language."[55]

Perhaps the difference between the various accounts of her sermon is that in one Truth *declares* she is a woman, while Gage cites the refrain "Arn't I a Woman?" as a question. The declarative over the interrogative, Margaret Washington claims, is "in keeping with [Truth's] defiant character."[56] The declarative also demands attention and asserts truth rather than asking a question for which the answer could be no, though it anticipates the answer as yes, rhetorically. Still, Truth, having been told no throughout her life, would not give an opportunity for white people to see her as less than.

In the sermon, Sojourner Truth pointed to the impossibility of Black women ever being considered fully human by the dominant white society. She brought to task the cult of domesticity, which claimed a proper woman was a white, upper-class woman.[57] Though she was not white or middle class, she had served as a wet nurse to her enslavers, remarking in another setting that her breasts "had suckled many a white babe."[58] In this setting, she pointed out that even breasts and her milk—the mark of motherhood—had not made her a woman according to their eyes.

Because she had been enslaved and was Black, she pointed out that no one ever "helped [her] into carriages."[59] Though a woman, she could do anything a man could do: "I have plowed, and planted, and gathered into barns, and no man could head me—and ar'n't I a woman? I could work as much and eat as much as a man (when I could get it), and bear de lash as well—and ar'n't a woman?"[60] This comment about her hard work was probably a reference to her memoir, published not long before she preached these words. Her *Narrative* tells of how her enslaver bragged that she could work harder than most men: "Her master insisted that she could do as much work as half a dozen common people, and do it well, too."[61] That Truth could be superhuman, exceeding expectations, performing the tasks of both men and women, and still not be granted full and equal rights, pointed to the hypocrisy of advocating for the rights of white women rather than all women.

During the sermon, Truth asked the audience, some of whom were skeptical about women's rights and ability to vote, "What did your Christ come from? God and a woman. Man had nothing to do with him!" She continues, "If [the first] woman God ever made was strong enough to turn the world upside down, all 'lone, [these women] . . . ought to be able to turn it back and get it right side up again."[62]

Here, the Spirit's withness in Truth shaped her exegesis of Scripture to demonstrate a hermeneutic that privileges women's, and specifically Black women's bodies, as holy.[63] Truth's creative rendering of the biblical character Eve—specifically, Eve's power—testified to the Spirit within examining the validity and use of Scriptures. God, who created Truth as a Black woman, was with her as she suffered the evils of slavery. For the audience, she bore witness not only to the cruelties of slavery but to the divine Spirit indwelling her in her exegesis of Eve. Not only could Truth do the work of both men and women, but she could also interpret Scripture, examine it in context, and apply it to her own setting. Such intellect and skill demanded Truth have the same rights as white men—since she could do every task they could do, and more.

Truth continued to detail the labor she had to work while enslaved. She bared her arm to the audience, demanding they look at her and look at her arm.[64] Her arm exposed the scars of her enslavement. She insisted they see her hand, which had suffered a disease twenty-four years earlier and was the reason Dumont refused to free her when he said he would.[65] Truth, proud of her body and all it could do, knew the injustice of refusing Black women the right to vote. Her body bore witness to the cruelties of slavery and patriarchy. Her body also demonstrated how the divine was with her, as she explained in her sermon when she cried,

"None but Jesus heard me."[66] The Holy Spirit, who was the Spirit of Jesus she saw in her vision at her conversion, was the same Spirit who groaned within her as she ached for her freedom. This groaning found its roots in Scripture: in Romans 8:23, the apostle Paul explained that all of creation and those who have the spirit "groan within ourselves, waiting for . . . the redemption of our body."[67]

Truth's sermon represented an act of vulnerability that also is resistance.[68] That is, the Spirit within her enabled her to be vulnerable. In turn, by revealing her vulnerability, she exposed the hypocrisy of those who would not offer Black women full and equal rights. She could have chosen not to speak after pushback from Jane Swisshelm and other white women who had said that Black women's speaking distracted from the convention's larger agenda.[69] She could have stepped back when men claimed that because Christ was a man, women did not deserve the same rights as men. Instead, Truth took the podium and demanded, in an act of vulnerability, for the audience to *look* at her and her scars. Truth's vulnerability was a testament to her withness to the horrors she had been subjected to by the men who said she was inferior. Truth exposed her arm in "Arn't I a Woman" as an act of vulnerability in order to demonstrate the violence done to her by people who would deny her rights. Truth named "what others seek to ignore or normalize," pointing out both white supremacy and misogyny, both of which held that she was inferior—or did not consider her at all. Truth's vulnerability in speaking her truth "is a practice of love, of tenderness"—of withnessing. By becoming vulnerable to the audience, she enabled them to empathize with her story, pressuring them to reconsider their position and blind spots. Her pride in her Black body and the show-ing of her scars was "a practice of calculated self-disclosure" that compelled her audience to be open to the Spirit's with-ness within her.[70]

Preaching to an African American Congregation

Sojourner Truth's understanding of the Spirit as withness means she preached and ministered with and to her fel-low African Americans, not just to white audiences. In one sermon she gave, speaking to Colored Congregational Church in New York City in 1853, she proclaimed God's Spirit had come upon her. Like her near-contemporary Zil-pha Elaw, she spoke of her weaknesses—her first language was Dutch, she was from rural New York, and she had been enslaved—yet God had helped her. Speaking to her own people, who knew firsthand racism and enslavement, the difficulty of preaching, she said that "she lived and God lived in her." At first, she was consumed by hatred of white people. She then proudly declared she "gloried her color" and "was well satisfied" with the "color that God had been pleased to give her." She encouraged Black women to demand all the rights to which they were entitled—not just emancipation and liberation from racism but also the right to vote. In this, she "exhorted the people to stir and not let the white people have it all to themselves." This sermon occurred the same year she gave her "Arn't I a Woman" sermon.[71]

Ten years later in Rochester, New York, Truth more boldly expressed her thankfulness that God created her Black. Lecturing during the Civil War, she claimed she was proud to be Black, and not white, because white people were "so guilty and cruel" to Black people. Truth also criticized Northern churches that opened the communion table to enslavers, claiming she would rather eat with pigs in the trough than receive communion with them. Her friend Frederick Douglass affirmed her sentiment, preferring to be Black and bear scars than identify with the cruelty of white people.[72] Her pride in her Blackness remained steadfast regardless of audience or issue. She manifested the image of God in her Black body.

The concept that "she lived and God lived in her" accounted for her experience of the Spirit's withness and God's presence with her in her enslavement and struggles. She also claimed her body, though weak and scarred, bore imprints of the divine, as "God pleased to give her" a Black body. God's pleasure in her body meant that she must fight for all of her rights as a Black woman. Her "glorying in her color" held erotic undertones, as she appreciated herself and her body as it was and saw her body as fully made in God's image. That statement also enabled the Black congregants to see themselves as made in God's image, worthy of claiming and fighting for their rights. Self-love for Truth enabled her to encourage others to love themselves, resisting white supremacy in the process. For Truth, mutuality and withnessing went hand in hand. As Kelly Oliver remarks, "Bearing witness [and withness —ed.], in this context, means not only listening to the other but also telling oneself to the other."[73] Truth does this as she constructs narratives of herself to tell others. In sharing her life and witness, including the Spirit's withness in her, she opens her life to others as a source of comfort and strength.[74]

Baring Her Breast

Truth not only opened up her life as a source of comfort but also did so to shame proslavery advocates, who saw her as less than human. Abolitionist William Hayward recounted that Truth gave a series of antislavery lectures in Northern Indiana in 1858. While Indiana was a free state, Hayward described it as a "border-ruffian" that appeared "to be jealous and suspicious of every anti-slavery movement."[75] Those who were proslavery began to spread a rumor that Truth was a man dressed as a woman and hired by the Republican party to lecture.[76] This rumor was an attempt to discredit her story and shame her. A Dr. T. W. Strain, whom Hayward identified as "a mouthpiece of the slave democracy," demanded that Truth reveal her breast to the women of the audience to crush the rumor.

Strain had bet forty dollars that Truth was not a woman and wanted to cash in. Strain and the other pro-slavery white men wanted to deny "her witness as an Abolitionist and her integrity as preacher-teacher. The white men wanted to substantiate the concept of black women as objects—whether free or enslaved—not, as they claimed, determine her gender."[77] Sojourner Truth refused them the opportunity to shame her. She told them that several white infants had nursed at her breasts, which had meant that her own children had not had enough milk. Though her breasts had nursed, she remarked that they "in her estimation, [were] far more manly than they [her persecutors] appeared to be." Staring down her accusers directly, she quietly opened her blouse and bared her breast. When a couple of young white men ogled her, she turned to them and asked if they too wanted to suck her breast.[78] By taking command of the situation, Truth felt the Spirit within her and with her in discrediting the white men who wanted to objectify her. The Spirit's withness sanctioned her to claim her authority as a Black woman whose powerful testimony and bodily presence shamed and mocked the white men present. She knew God had created her and that God's Spirit was within her. In this moment, she lived out Psalm 118:6: "The Lord is on my side; I will not fear: what can man do unto me?"[79]

The Spirit's Joyful Withness

Knowing the Lord was on her side and the Spirit was within her, Truth could lecture and preach joyfully. Truth's joy serves as an act of resistance against those who would deny her personhood. One way Truth lived joyfully was through song and musicality. While she was enslaved, she sang as she worked—creatively engaging her mind while completing repetitive and difficult tasks.[80] She expressed her joy even as she faced ridicule. She recalled a camp meeting where a group of rowdy men descended, intending to disrupt her and the meeting. She noticed she was the only Black person there and feared for her life. With that fear accompanying her, she got up to preach and began to sing about the resurrection. Gilbert remarked, "The hymn, the tune, the style, are each too closely associated with to be easily separated from herself, and when sung in one of her most animated moods, in the open air, with the utmost strength of her most powerful voice, must have been truly thrilling."[81] Filled with the Holy Spirit, she calmed the potential rioters with her music, asserting her joy even as they tried to stoke her (and the audience's) fear.

Later, as a freedwoman and prominent lecturer, she opened many lectures with song and peppered them with music.[82] Several witnesses to her lectures describe her deep powerful voice and her as "greatly moved by the Spirit." One newspaper remarked, "Her voice rings like a clarion," loud and powerful, full of confidence and assurance. She composed and sold her songs at her lectures.[83] Frances Titus, who compiled and edited the second edition of Truth's *Narrative*, adding "A Book of Life," described her voice as both "sweet and powerful," prompting "cheer after cheer." Her bodily presence "moved the audience to laughter and tears."[84] Truth utilizes music as a way to express joy, and the outpouring of the Holy Spirit within her.

Sometimes, for Truth, a sense of humor indicated her joy. She was the first Black woman to lecture in the Northampton commune in 1844.[85] In one meeting, she once quipped, "Three thirds of the people are wrong." Someone soon shouted back, "That takes them all, Sojourner." Quick on her feet, she retorted back, "I am sorry. I had hoped there were a few left."[86] While this could be considered a misspoken statement on her part, the humorous exchange indicated her broader views on human nature. In an era where prejudice against Black people was sanctioned by law, and where women were expected to conform to Victorian ideals, even as working-class and poor women struggled to make ends meet, Truth saw her statement as accurate. As she examined those around her, she felt much like Frederick Douglass in his comments on Christianity: "I can see no reason, but the most deceitful one, for calling the religion of this land Christianity."[87] Truth's humor revealed her feelings as a Black woman living in the United States.

Toward the end of her 1850 narrative, Truth is shown deploying humor in her relationship with her former enslaver, John Dumont. Olive Gilbert depicts an event where Truth, in visiting her daughter Diana, also encounters Dumont. Diana had some sort of chronic illness and thus stayed near Dumont because she had no place to care for her. Truth, in seeing Dumont for the first time in a while, depicted him as "advanced in age, and reduced in property." Dumont, in his frail state, seemed to have a change in heart, saying now that "slavery was the wickedest thing in the world," though, while he enslaved people, he did not think anything of it. Truth wondered with him if present enslavers might have a similar mindset—seeing slavery as normal and people as property. Dumont promptly answered no: "For, now, the sin of slavery is so clearly written out, and so much talked against,—(why, the whole world cries out against it!)—that if any one says he don't know, and has not heard, he must, I think, be a liar." Truth seemed unconvinced of his optimism. In her travels and experience as a Black woman, enslavers—and indeed, many other white people—still possessed a hardness of heart. Gilbert, Truth's recorder, cites Zechariah 7:11: "They have stopped their ears that they may not hear."[88] Dumont, now without the power he once held, may have felt that everyone was against enslavement, but states that still upheld slavery proved otherwise. Further, Dumont was required to free enslaved persons in New York after a certain date, so he could look back on his enslaving days with regret. Truth probably wondered whether, if this was not the requirement, he would have continued to enslave people.

Truth ultimately received the last laugh when it came to her enslaver. She received a letter in 1849 from Diana. Diana relayed to her that her enslaver had "gone west" with some of his sons and, in doing so, had also taken some of Truth's furniture, probably by mistake. Truth was not bothered by it, remarking, "Never mind . . . what we give to the poor, we lend to the Lord." In this final comment, in the closing of her narrative, Truth points out how Dumont, who once enslaved her, had become a recipient of her charity: "[Truth] recalled the lectures he used to give his slaves, on speaking the truth and being honest, and laughing, she says he taught us not to lie and steal, when he was stealing all the time himself."[89] The last sentence of the narrative opens with "poor old man," followed by a thankfulness for his change of heart, even if it was too little too late. The roles had reversed. Truth's inclusion of her former enslaver is a real example of Matthew 23:12: "All who exalt themselves will be humbled, and all who humble themselves will be exalted."

Truth's humor also came in the form of parables. One journalist describes a speech she gave following the Dred Scott decision, the same decision that Julia Foote referenced in her autobiography. Truth had compared the boll weevil, a pest that destroys crops, to the Supreme Court decision authored by Justice Taney that declared Black people had no rights that the government was bound to respect:

"Children, I talks to God and God talks to me," she said. "Dis morning I was walking out, and I got over de fence. I saw de wheat a holding up its head, looking very big." Her powerful deep voice rose as she emphasized VERY BIG, drew up to full height, and pretending to grab a stalk of wheat, she discovered "dere was no wheat dare!" She asked God, "What is de matter wid dis wheat?" And he says to me, "Sojourner, dere is a little weasel [*sic*] in it." Likewise, hearing all about the Constitution and rights of man, she said, "I comes up and I takes hold of dis Constitution."[90]

Truth likened the pesty, destructive boll weevil to the Supreme Court, which, in the Dred Scott decision, had gone against the Declaration of Independence, which stated "that all men are created equal, that they are endowed by their Creator with certain unalienable Rights, that among these are Life, Liberty and the pursuit of Happiness."[91] However, when Truth spoke to God about the Constitution, asking God, "What ails dis Constitution?" God responded in Sojourner's voice, "Sojourner, dere is a little weasel [*sic*] in it." The most powerful court in the nation had been reduced to a pesky bug. Truth's storytelling power testified to the withness of the Holy Spirit just as much as her words. One observer described Truth's presence as a "magnetic power" that not only captivated her audience but convinced them of her cause.[92] Her presence and gestures heightened the absurdity of the Supreme Court's decision and were both humorous and full of truth.

Withness as a Source of Power

In addition to seeing the Spirit's withness as a source of joy that included humor, Sojourner Truth understood the Spirit's withness to be a source of power. She practiced this during a meeting in Battle Creek, Michigan, which became her home in her later life. During the Civil War, white supremacist violence pervaded the Northern states. The North placed blame on Black people for the Civil War and, as a result, committed acts of violence against them. In Detroit in March of 1863, white people falsely accused a Black man of hurting a white woman. While authorities convicted the man and sentenced him to life in prison, this did not stop white mobs from rioting in Black neighborhoods and harassing any white people who attempted to help the Black people who were harmed. Three months after the riots, a Sunday school convention in Detroit took place for a mostly white audience. Of all the participants, only one person addressed the current events at hand, specifically speaking about racism. On the last day, they held a service especially for children, which Sojourner Truth attended. Truth, bored with the loquacious speeches that failed to hold the children's attention, asked if she could say something. After she was recognized as a preacher and lecturer, she was permitted to speak.

She asked the children who made their skin white. They replied that it was God. She then asked them who made her skin black. They responded in kind: God did. She then said that it was "a reproach upon our Maker to despise a part of his children because he has been pleased to give them a black skin." She told her mostly white audience of children that their teachers must "root up, if possible, the great sin of prejudice against color from your minds." Addressing the children directly, she chastised them, "Get rid of your prejudice and learn to love [Black] children."[93] She testified to the Holy Spirit within her, bearing witness to the dignity of Black bodies and the injustice of white supremacy. God created both Black and white children in God's image; thus, they should be treated equally.

The Spirit's witness empowered her still as she demanded equality not only in the church and the voting booth but also in public transportation. During and after the Civil War, Truth was appointed to the Freedman's Hospital in Washington, DC, as an attendant, nursing sick soldiers, veterans, and Black refugees with contagious diseases exacerbated by limited treatments and poor living conditions.[94] She would often have to walk long distances to retrieve supplies for them, as the streetcars were segregated. Though the streetcars generally had a "Jim Crow" car for Black people, it was often filled with white people, who demanded Black people stand. Truth complained to the streetcar authorities, who abolished the Jim Crow car and integrated (in theory) the streetcars. But in one instance, when Truth indicated to the conductor that she wanted to hop aboard, he ignored her. She yelled loudly to get his attention: "I want to ride!! I want to ride!!" A hush came over the streetcar and the surrounding streets, as observers were amazed at Truth's outburst. Still, the conductor ignored her. So Truth, in her mid sixties, jumped aboard the streetcar when it had stopped. When the conductor demanded she get out, she retorted "that she was neither a Marylander nor a Virginian to fear his threats; but was from the Empire State of New York, and knew the laws as well as he did."[95] She rode beyond her destination, glorying in her victory against the white conductor. The Spirit within her had expelled any fear of injury as she boarded the car, shaming its white conductor in the process.

Conclusion: A Style That Defies Imitation

Sojourner Truth's later years testified to the Spirit's witness. She continued her mission for both full equality of Black people and the right for women to vote. She advocated for formerly enslaved Black people to move west to Kansas for better opportunities. In her seventies and eighties, she still spoke to congregations and assemblies. She spoke in a way "that defie[d] imitation."[96] At age eighty-three, she explained her faith to an audience: "She feels that [God] is all around her; that we live in [God] as the fishes live in the sea."[97] Her life and witness exemplified such words. The Spirit's witness had sustained her during her enslavement and compelled her to walk away from her master. At her conversion, she had seen no place where God was not, echoing Psalm 139:7: "Whither shall I go from thy spirit? or whither shall I flee from thy presence?"[98] When she ached for her son, she knew God ached with her. When others attempted to shame her, she testified to the Spirit within her by exposing their sin. Her life, words, and witness confirmed, in the words of Ephesians 3:16, the God who strengthened her "inner being with power through [God's] Spirit."

5

Black Women Preachers as Exemplars of a Prophetic Pastoral Theology

Foote, Elaw, and Truth's sermons and narratives demonstrate the power of theology to celebrate freedom and indict oppression. Their stories also present a nuanced understanding of the God who loves them and their communities. All three women displayed the foolishness of God, bodied the Word, and developed an understanding of the Spirit as witness. Within their theologies, a Trinitarian theme arises: the foolishness of God intuits the First Person, bodying the Word associates with the Second, and witness of the Spirit with the Third. The interconnectedness of the themes correlates with the interconnected nature of triune life. In embracing and practicing all three motifs, the women become pastoral prophets, speaking the good news to a world that denies them authority or personhood.

For Elaw, Foote, and Truth, to be pastoral was to be prophetic. As the women preached a word of comfort to the oppressed, the privileged would have heard judgment in their voices. White supremacy and misogyny had been made into a false religion. Elaw implied she knew more than the enslavers' educated ministers, Foote refused to preach in places that limited access to Black people, and Sojourner Truth called out particular white men for inconsistencies in their theologies. Together, these women present a soteriology concerned with whole persons and whole communities. This soteriology is mystically contemplative, fosters empathy, and honors their own bodies and the bodies of those to whom they preach.

Why the Pastoral Is Prophetic and the Prophetic Is Pastoral

Elaw, Foote, and Truth perceive the prophetic in the vein of the prophets in the Hebrew Scriptures. They cite these prophets numerous times in their sermons and autobiographies. Hebrew prophets saw themselves as called by God, sent to speak the Word to their communities. Their messages could be directives, pronouncements of judgment or wrath, or even comforting words. The Hebrew root word for prophet, *navi*, describes either the one who calls or the one who is called.[1] In the Hebrew Scriptures, prophets were not lone individuals but members of the larger community who were accountable to the society. The twentieth-century Jewish mystic Abraham Heschel perceives the prophetic as siding with the downtrodden, expressing both anger and sympathy: "Prophecy is the voice that God has lent to the silent agony, a voice to the plundered."[2] The three women, in different ways, body this voice of God to their communities. They all document their experiences of racism and sexism. Sojourner Truth, for example, spoke of the exploitation of her enslaved Black siblings. They make the silent agony visible in their sermons and memoirs.

Elaw, Foote, and Truth functioned pastorally in that they offered care and support to their audiences and communities, helping people draw closer to God. The sixth-century theologian Gregory the Great, who wrote the first pastoral care manual, describes a good pastor as one who is "a near neighbour to every one in sympathy, and exalted above all in contemplation."[3] For Gregory, a pastor must both possess good integrity and love their neighbors. Gregory's description of a pastor infers that Jesus Christ is the ultimate pastor, who, like a shepherd, cares for his flock by speaking truth. Jesus as the Good Shepherd loves and protects his flock.[4] Elaw, Foote, and Truth bodied this pastoral presence as well: speaking a prophetic word to oppressors meant promoting the well-being of the downtrodden. The pastoral and prophetic necessarily interconnect for all women.

Mystically Contemplative: Reflecting upon God

Elaw, Foote, and Truth saw mystical contemplation as a time set apart to ponder how God works in their lives. They would reflect on themselves and their callings while contemplating themselves as made in the divine image, interrogating their experience with God and others, asking God for guidance and wisdom, or stepping away for critical self-discernment. Self-reflection serves as a tool of change and an opportunity for sanctification. All three women see self-reflection as involving an assertion of selfhood ordained by God in resistance to a patriarchal and white supremacist system.

Contemplation

The twentieth-century African American mystic Howard Thurman describes the need for contemplation like this: "[One] can become at home within by locating in [their] own spirit the trysting place where [they] and God may meet. Here it is that life may become private, personal, without at the same time becoming self-centered. . . . Here the individual comes to [themselves], the wanderer comes home, and the private life is saved for deliberate involvement."[5] Elaw, Foote, and Truth perceived contemplation as necessary for their well-being and what enabled them to receive visions.

When Zilpha Elaw heard both her sister and another woman express that they saw her called by God to preach, she created space within her soul inwardly: "I kept these things very reservedly to myself; as did Mary the mother of Christ." Facing her husband's antagonism, Elaw "contemplat[ed] the wonderful works of creation, or revelation of the mind and truth of God to [humanity]."[6] Julia Foote felt a call to preach similar to Elaw's, and met it with resistance. She "took all [her] doubts and fears to the Lord in prayer." In that moment of prayer and contemplation, she saw an angel who wrote, "Thee have I chosen to preach my Gospel without delay."[7] Sojourner Truth contemplated her faith as she grew: "[Her views], which were the results of the workings of her own mind were, for a long time after their adoption, closely locked in her own breast."[8] Truth wrestled with theological concepts prior to publicly preaching on them, "locking" them inside her. All three women see their inner selves as a place to meet God safely, to learn from God and to learn about God, and to receive divine visions. In their contemplation, they created a safe space to voice their doubts and griefs. Their contemplative practices with God enabled them to accept themselves as divinely called to preach and minister.

Mysticism

Contemplation and mysticism intertwine—in order to contemplate, one must embrace mysticism. Thurman perceives mysticism as "the response of the individual to a personal encounter with God within [their] own spirit. Such a response is total, affecting the inner quality of the life and its outward expression and manifestation."[9] While Thurman emphasizes that one cannot provide empirical evidence or data for the mystical experience, one's inner life should match one's outer life. He gives the example of the Society of Friends, or the Quakers. Founded by George Fox in the seventeenth century, Quakerism emphasizes the "inner light" of the Spirit to illumine one's understanding. From their founding, Quakers were known for supporting women's preaching and for their antislavery stance.[10] Their religious beliefs exemplify how mystical contemplation leads to praxis. For instance, Sojourner Truth turned to the Quakers to help get her son back after he was sold into slavery.[11] Zilpha Elaw was told to leave the Methodists and join the Quakers, as they had always allowed women's preaching.[12] Elaw, Foote, and Truth's mystical experiences pointed to both the greatness of God and their own finitude in light of God.[13] And yet, despite their finitude, they saw themselves as especially ordained and called by the divine. The immanent and transcendent collided in their mystical experience, and the women found themselves in the middle.

Largely, studies in mysticism focus upon European medieval or monastic figures, exposing a whiteness that appears prevalent in studies on Christian mysticism. However, Black people in the African diaspora have always engaged in mystical practices, though their categories might look different from the white Western European tradition.[14] Nonetheless, Black and womanist theologians claim and theologize Black mystical experience and discern mysticism in their heroes of faith. For instance, Margaret Washington describes Truth's mother's spirituality as an interweaving of "Christianity and African mysticism."[15] She calls Truth an "African Dutch mystic" to honor Truth's spiritual roots and her orientation to the divine.[16] Barbara Ann Holmes describes Martin Luther King Jr., Fannie Lou Hamer, Rosa Parks, and Howard Thurman as "public mystics." Holmes identifies "public mystics" as those whose "interiority and communal reference points intersect."[17] This appears common for Black mystics. Foote, Elaw, and Truth embraced mysticism in that they understood their bodies as places where the divine could meet them. They did not rely on

Scripture alone in encountering the divine but also used the knowledge of their own bodies, their families' experiences, and the events around them. For them, mystical living and contemplation were ways of being in the world and not things done only in private or in church.[18]

Undergirded in the mystical tradition is the concept of not-knowing (apophasis), which connects to the medieval mystic Meister Eckhart's concept of "God beyond God."[19] While, on one hand, the women received special visions and, therefore, special knowledge from God, they knew there were always new depths of the divine to explore. For example, Sojourner Truth embraced apophasis when she exclaimed in her conversion, "God, I did not know you were so big!"[20] Foote, when she was converted, describes being "filled with rapture too deep for words."[21] As Elaw sailed across the Atlantic to England, she imagined all the fish in the ocean and the birds of the air and marveled at the vastness of God's creation.[22] In these women, embracing apophasis provoked awe and wonder, which in turn caused them to turn more fully to God. Their embrace of God's hiddenness meant they knew they could grow and learn in both knowledge of God and knowledge of themselves.

Honoring Bodiliness

Truth, Foote, and Elaw knew deep within from their practices of mystical contemplation that their bodies were created in the image and likeness of God. Throughout their lives, they affirmed their bodies as particularly holy. They tapped into what Black feminist Audre Lorde calls an "erotic power."[23] This erotic power is not primarily or only sexual but instead sees the "deepest feelings" the women experience as a source of powerful knowledge.[24] They honored their bodies, and the knowledge, strength, and wisdom their bodies held. Tapping into their erotic power allowed them to define themselves not as inferior, as the world saw them, but as they viewed themselves: as reflections of the divine. Their erotic power can be perceived as intuition or a gut feeling, guiding their behaviors and actions. Because they were in touch with their erotic power, they listened to their bodies.

Zilpha Elaw tapped into her deepest feelings and relayed them to a congregation where she was preaching in Hartford, Connecticut. The chapel officials, who had originally promised she would preach in the afternoon, went back on their promise as she prepared to enter the church. Following their direction, she unhappily sat with the congregation. However, when the deacons of the church saw her with the congregation, they begged her to come forward and preach from the pulpit anyway. Upon ascending to the pulpit, before "she could utter a word," she broke down in tears in front of the congregation. She felt the weight of being dismissed again and again in her body, which manifested in her tears. Once she finished crying, she preached a powerful sermon. She returned to worship that evening and listened to the appointed preacher deliver his own. However, afterward, the congregation remained in their seats, "maintained a profound silence," and looked at Elaw. Elaw, intuiting they wanted her to say something, got up and offered to conduct a prayer meeting at that moment. Before she could say another word, the officials took over, "without deigning the least notice of [her]," and would not let her preach.[25] Elaw wanted to care for the congregation but also knew she could not care for them unless the authorities acknowledged her pastoral presence as a Black woman. Thus, she listened to her gut intuition and did not preach there again until several months later, when she was welcomed with open arms. She respected herself and her body enough to refuse to be treated as less than.

Julia Foote honored her body to the point that she ran away after Mrs. Prime whipped her. Mrs. Prime, her mistress for a time when she was a girl, accused Foote of stealing pound cakes. While Foote was innocent, Mrs. Prime did not believe her. One day, after the Primes returned home from town, Mrs. Prime took a rawhide and beat Foote's back. When Foote pled her innocence, Mrs. Prime eventually put the rawhide away, promising to whip Foote the following day until she confessed. That afternoon, while Mrs. Prime was away, Foote took the rawhide, chopped it up into tiny pieces, and threw them out of eyesight. Then the next morning before the sun rose, Foote left the Primes and walked back to her parents' home. She described the journey as "a long, lonely road through the woods," where every sound frightened her and made her think someone was following her. When Foote reached her parents, she explained to her mother all that had happened. Her mother, upon meeting with the Primes that afternoon, spoke to them about the whipping. Foote, with her mother's prodding, reluctantly returned to them. Thankfully, "they were as kind to me as ever."[26] As a girl, Foote listened to her body's pain and knew it was against what God wanted for her. She gave up what Lorde describes as "being satisfied with suffering and self-negation, and with the numbness" that would have let her accept the beating as normal or OK.[27] Because she embraced her bodily autonomy and loved herself, she could resist Mrs. Primes's dehumanization of her.

Sojourner Truth resisted anyone who denied her full and equal rights. In honoring her bodiliness, she advocated for all Black women's bodies. Invited to speak at the 1867 American Equal Rights Association, Truth knew she was up against more than her fair share of detractors. White women suffragists did not also advocate for Black men's right to vote, claiming Black men's oppression inhibited them from exercising the proper judgment in voting. White women argued against Black men's suffrage in favor of their own. After receiving applause from the audience when she stepped on the stage, Truth quipped, "I don't know how you will feel when I get through."[28] She insisted Black women needed their rights just as much as Black men and white women. In having equal rights, Black women would be able to keep the money they earned, own property, and become independent. For Truth, a woman of seventy years old, to keep the money she earned would allow her to be cared for in her old age. In the aftermath of the Civil War and amid renewed interest in suffrage, Truth urged, "I am for keeping the thing going while things are stirring; because if we wait till it is still, it will take a great while to get it going again."[29] More than twenty years after she had delivered her "Arn't I a Woman" sermon, Truth still pushed for full rights for Black women. Keeping in line with Lorde's work on erotic power, Truth "[became] less willing to accept powerlessness, resignation, despair, self-effacement, depression, self-denial." Truth refused to give up as she honored her body in advocating for her full rights. By honoring her own bodiliness, she also honored all people's bodies—Black and white, rich and poor. Truth, Foote, and Elaw, as Audre Lorde puts it, "grow beyond whatever distortions [they] may find within [themselves that keep them] docile and loyal and obedient, externally defined, and leads [them] to accept many facets of [their] oppression as women."[30]

Relational Empathy: The Spirit Within

The Spirit within Zilpha Elaw, Sojourner Truth, and Julia Foote fostered in them a sense of empathy toward those to whom they ministered. *Empathy* means to feel with or "in" another person and can be identified as "an imaginative identification with another's existential situation." This "imaginative identification" requires emotional intelligence, as the women sought to understand their context and preach a word their audiences needed to hear.[31] Truth, Elaw, and Foote all "felt with" their audiences as they traveled and preached. Their empathy strengthened their pastoral prophetic presence.

Elaw demonstrated her empathy in her one-on-one interactions as she traveled. She would often spend hours with people who were sick, dying, or in need of extra spiritual support. She saw her ministry with them as just as important as her pulpit appearances with full crowds. After a full preaching schedule, Elaw had made preparations to return to Manchester. When she stopped to say good-bye to a Mrs. H., Mrs. H. expressed disappointment, for she had felt "very burdened" spiritually. Mrs. H. began to cry.

Elaw, seeing her distress, "needed no further persuasion to stay."[32] Under Elaw's caring ministry, Mrs. H. found assurance in Christ and peace in her soul. Elaw had empathized with Mrs. H.'s emotional distress and changed her schedule to be and feel with her. In another instance, toward the end of her *Memoirs*, Elaw prayed with one young woman on her deathbed. The young woman, although unable to speak, took Elaw's hand, and looked at her with an "affectionately languishing smile."[33] Elaw felt a connection with the woman and was glad to provide her with spiritual encouragement on her deathbed.

Julia Foote's empathy shone when she advocated for other Black women preachers. In the middle of her ministry, she traveled to Philadelphia for a church meeting of area African Methodist Episcopal pastors and laypeople. Philadelphia was where Richard Allen had left St. George's church. Foote met three other women who, like her, felt called to itinerant ministry. They had received so much pushback that they "were very much distressed and shrank from their duty." Even worse, the harshest criticism they received was from their area ministers. This stung Foote deeply. After all, when she had traveled to Philadelphia, she had felt a spiritual relationship with the ministers: "My heart went out in love to each of them as though he had been my father." If they were of the secular world, Foote would not have taken the men's criticism so deeply. But the criticism came from the ministers, "from those who had been much—blessed—blessed with [Foote] and who had once been friends of mine, it touched a tender spot." The fond feelings she had for the ministers had been shaken by their cruelty in prohibiting her newfound friends' ministerial gifts. Foote suggested to the women that they hold a series of meetings where the women could use their pastoral abilities. A meeting was like a Bible study led by a mentor with a mature faith. The women assented to the idea as long as Foote led it. Foote rented a large place for eleven days, which stayed full every night with participants. Some people who attended the class meetings were there to mock them, including the ministers. One of her fellow women preachers, stressed by the ridicule, left after two days, afraid she would be excommunicated. Foote did not blame the woman for her early departure; she blamed it on the sins of her accusers.[34] Foote, who had empathized with the ministers as she traveled, now felt with her Black sisters who also wanted to preach. She understood their pain because she had experienced the same criticisms. She chose to align herself not with the more powerful ministers but with the women who had no standing. Foote's empathy emboldened her to take matters into her own hands in creating a space where the women could exercise their gifts.

Sojourner Truth solicited empathy from her audience to get them to agree to her cause. The stories she included in her *Narrative* were meant to arouse compassion from the readers. In evoking empathy for herself, she hoped to garner empathy from whites for all Black people who had suffered a life like hers. In addition, telling her own stories and experiences allowed her to empathize with her fellow Black people, who had experienced enslavement and suffering at the hands of whites. She felt with her young son Peter as she traced the scars on his back, remembering the pain that caused her own scars and hand injury. Truth also aroused empathy on the abolitionist lecture circuit. She listened to speakers debating the notion of American Union—that is, states' rights to develop their own laws while remaining associated with the larger federal government. People who advocated for the idea of an American Union either accepted slavery as a compromise or were actively supportive of it. Quietly, Truth remarked "she knew something of Union—she had felt it; the scars of it were on her back, and she would carry them to her grave. Union was not sweet to her."[35] Here, she voiced what so many Black Americans were thinking: white people who advocated for unity at the expense of enslavement, or gradual emancipation, did not know or feel with the suffering of Black people. Truth's comments stirred the feelings of her audience, turning them to Truth's side.

For all three women, their empathy allowed them to become vulnerable, opening up their lives and withness to the world around them. They saw their ability to "feel with" people as a gift of the Spirit within them. This Spirit was the same one the apostle Paul says "intercedes with sighs too deep for words."[36] This was the Spirit of Jesus Christ, who in his incarnation, death, and resurrection was "[able] to sympathize with [their] weaknesses," their hurts, and their joys.[37]

An Interconnected Conclusion: Theory and Praxis

For the pastorally prophetic Foote, Elaw, and Truth, their theologies prove theory and praxis necessarily connect. They did not have the privilege of a seminary education or the time to write theological treatises, yet their astute minds took white theology to task. Simultaneously, as a result of their Methodist roots, as they learned, they grew, adapted, and sharpened their theologies to speak to their context. One can chart a movement toward a holier, more socially active divine life in their narratives. This movement is what Nancy Bedford describes as a "theological hermeneutical spiral," whereby the process of discerning one's actions and beliefs includes encountering reality, exposing harmful beliefs, and reevaluating resources. One can enter the spiral at any moment; the process of spiraling never ceases. The goal of the spiral is to discern the heart of the Trinitarian, loving God.[38] Sojourner Truth's description of her faith development—from inheriting her mother's religion to preaching the lecture circuit—attested to such a spiral as she discerned her calling. As historian Nell Irvin Painter remarks, Sojourner Truth did not have a singular identity; but as she lived her life as a freed person away from slavery, she had to learn and grow.[39]

The same could be said for Elaw and Foote. Their accounts detail temptation, mistakes, or struggles. Even after their sanctification, they sometimes experienced a dark night of the soul, wondering if God had really called them and if their ministries would continue to bear fruit. Their journeys detailed them trusting the Spirit's sanctifying work within them and within the world. Their ministries reflect what Paul proclaims: that "[our] love may overflow more and more with knowledge and full insight to help [us] to determine what is best"—for both others and ourselves.[40]

That Love May Overflow:
Storied Witness for Today

Sojourner Truth, Zilpha Elaw, and Julia Foote lived in a time when Black women had no rights to life, liberty, and the pursuit of happiness. Today, while improvements have happened, the United States still treats Black women as inferior across the board. When it comes to job and economic equity, Black women earn 63 percent of the wages that white men do, and statistics do not improve significantly even with increased education. White women, on the other hand, earn 78.7 percent of the wages that white men do. Black women have the highest participation in the labor force and also were the most affected financially by the pandemic that began in March 2020.[41] In the political realm, in 2021, women of color made up 9.2 percent of Congress's 535 members, a new record. Of those women of color, twenty-three Black women served the House of Representatives, while no Black women served the Senate.[42] The legacy of enslavement and sexism that Elaw, Foote, and Truth fought against continues into the twenty-first century in persistent wage gaps, job precarity, and representation in government.

In church representation, Black women fare no better. Elaw, Foote, and Truth all associated with or were members of Methodist congregations throughout their lives and, as Black women, faced discrimination in pay and ministering opportunities. While women, both Black and white, have made gains in some settings, Black women face a disproportionate amount of sexism. In a 2014 analysis of United Methodist clergy, Black women represented

2.15 percent of total clergy, whereas white women stood for 21.65 percent of clergy.[43] White men, on the other hand, were 61.6 percent of all clergy. In the Evangelical Lutheran Church of America, 45.3 percent of women clergy of color indicated that they were paid less than synod guidelines.[44] Some historically Black denominations like the African Methodist Episcopal Church and the Christian Methodist Episcopal Church have seen an uptick of women in ministry that corresponds with white mainline denominations. However, in Black Baptist churches, women hold less than 10 percent of leadership or pastoral roles. This corresponds with predominantly white Baptist denominations like the Southern Baptist Convention, which has no women of any ethnicity as senior pastors.[45]

These inequities matter because the triune God created Black women in God's image, and to deny that image denies the living God. Elaw, Foote, and Truth refused to be denied their image-bearing status, expressively stating how God sent *them* to preach words of comfort and criticism. Black theologians follow in their footsteps today. In 2020, Black theologians delivered a statement on Juneteenth[46] in response to high-profile extrajudicial murders of Black people, which sparked national conversations and a wave of protests. To name just a few instances from 2020 alone, Ahmaud Arbery was murdered while running, police murdered George Floyd after they suspected him of using a counterfeit $20 bill, and Breonna Taylor was asleep when plainclothes officers entered her apartment and shot her. The statement, signed by almost seven hundred Black clergy and theologians, rejected "police brutality, militarism, and every form of state-sanctioned violence deployed under the banner of 'law and order' that disproportionately targets and aims to ravage Black life."[47] Reflecting on the 2020 Juneteenth statement, womanist theologian Eboni Marshall Turman emphasizes, "We have to tell that history for people who think that it doesn't exist, for people who think that their heritage is something that's disassociated from the current moment."[48]

The heritage of enslavement, state-sanctioned violence, and white supremacy runs deep—existing long before the founding of the United States. The heritage of Black women's resistance to such sins runs deeper. Foote, Elaw, and Truth offer a heritage rooted in love of oneself and love of one's neighbor. Theirs is the heritage of intense wrestling with Scripture. Their legacies depict a God who suffered with them but did not want them to remain in their suffering. Their storied witness offers theologies concerned with their world and gives insight into a twenty-first-century one as well.

Acknowledgments

If I were to express my gratitude to everyone properly, my thanksgiving would be longer than the book itself. I thank the women whose work inspired this book: Margaret Washington, Kimberly Blockett, and Joy Bostic. I am deeply indebted to their witness, as their theologizing, historical research, and literary studies shaped my own reading of Zilpha Elaw, Sojourner Truth, and Julia Foote. To my doctoral advisor Dr. Nancy Bedford—thank you for taking a chance on me, for modeling pastoral prophecy in your teaching and scholarship, and for challenging me to read widely and deeply. You encourage me to be myself and to see the task of theology as an act of loving God and loving my neighbor. My professors and dissertation committee members, Dr. Linda Thomas, Dr. Anne Joh, and Dr. Tim Eberhart—thank you for your rigorous and graceful instruction. You were compassionate in my vulnerabilities, provided space for me to test my ideas, and illuminated my blind spots. I am grateful.

For my Garrett Evangelical colleagues and their families, who have since become dear friends: thank you for your generous hospitality. To name only a few: Andrew Wymer and Jonathan Lemaster-Smith read and critiqued my work, recommended texts, and sent calls for papers my way. Christopher Hunt as my doctoral sibling has been my constant friend in the shaping of this work, from our meeting at our first doctoral class to my final edits on the book. He recommended texts and challenged me to think deeply and critically. Michele Watkins, Kristen Daley-Mosier, Jennifer Moe, Catherine Knott, Kerri Allen, and Elyssa Salinas-Lazarski were thoughtful dialogue partners and helped me understand difficult concepts.

Thank you also to the National Association of Baptist Professors of Religion, where I received a dissertation scholarship that enabled me to travel to present papers connected with this book and allowed me to develop friendships with fellow Baptist academics.

Multiple faith communities formed me and enabled this book to happen. Centertown Baptist Church and First Baptist Church of Jefferson City, Missouri, taught me the stories of faith and nurtured my calling to ministry. Holmeswood Baptist Church in Kansas City, Missouri, ordained me and blessed me to pursue PhD studies and write books. I am grateful for Keith Herron and Kathy Pickett, as they mentored me in ministry and sat with me as

I discerned graduate education. Dayspring Baptist Church provided faith and emotional support when I doubted and struggled. My current faith community, First St. Charles United Methodist Church, has embraced me with open arms, values my scholarship and ministry, and has been an overall blessing to my life. Thanks to Bart Hildreth, who covenanted with me to finish my PhD as I began my service there, and for the clergy and staff who took up the reigns when I needed to write. Thank you also to my amazing students, whose intelligence and humor continue to replenish my hope. You are the best.

Several friends and family accompanied me on this writing journey. Eileen Campbell-Reed's writing table, and the friendships cultivated therein, made this work happen, even when I was afraid and felt overwhelmed. My conversations with Laura Levens, Travis McMaken, and Lauren Larkin about our respective works helped me emphasize the importance of lifting up women as theologians. The friendships I made within the Young Clergywomen project and the St. Louis Shut Up and Write group sustained me with humor and grace. Thank you to Gail Aurand, Jeni Dancer, Crystal Baker, and Joy Jones for giving me a safe space to be myself. It feels impossible to thank my family. My siblings James and Maggie have been a steady source of support and confidence when I needed it. My parents provided meals and a quiet place to write, transported me to conferences, prayed for me, and offered feedback on my work. They nurtured my curiosity and loved me well, believing in me when I could not. A special thank you to my spouse and partner, Steve. You endured long stretches of my absence, listened to my anxieties, and brought me coffee as I typed. Even now, you sit quietly reading across the table as I work, giving me the space to think while assuring me with your presence. I love you.

This book is dedicated to the women it features: Zilpha Elaw, Julia Foote, and Sojourner Truth. May their memories continue to bless and teach us for years to come.

Notes

Preface

1 The Cooperative Baptist Fellowship lovingly refers to itself as a "denom-inetwork," combining *denomination* and *network*.

2 I will explain why scholars think it's "Arn't I a Woman" instead of "Ain't I a Woman?" in the chapter on Sojourner Truth.

3 Karen Teel, *Racism and the Image of God* (New York: Palgrave Macmillan, 2010), 9.

4 Teel, 9–10.

Chapter 1: Learning from Subverted Stories

1 Zilpha Elaw, *Memoirs of the Life, Religious Experience, Ministerial Travels, and Labours of Mrs. Elaw* (1846), in *Sisters of the Spirit: Three Black Women's Autobiographies of the Nineteenth Century*, ed. William L. Andrews (Bloomington: Indiana University Press, 1986), 72–74. Throughout the present volume, more than one version of sources for Elaw and Truth will be cited; as such, the year of publication will be provided in all subsequent citations to such sources for clarity.

2 Julia Foote, *A Brand Plucked from the Fire: An Autobiographical Sketch* (New York: George Hughes, 1879), 66.

3 Foote, 68.

4 Sojourner Truth, *Narrative of Sojourner Truth*, comp. Olive Gilbert (Boston:

published for author, 1850), "The Cause of Her Leaving the City." The phrase "the hope that was within her" is probably an allusion to 1 Pet 3:15, which, in the King James Version of the Bible, which was used in the United States, says, "But sanctify the Lord God in your hearts: and be ready always to give an answer to every man that asketh you a reason of the hope that is in you."

5 Margaret Washington, *Sojourner Truth's America* (Urbana: University of Illinois Press, 2009), loc. 6107, Kindle.

6 1 Cor 9:22.

7 Kimberlé Crenshaw, "Demarginalizing the Intersection of Race and Sex: A Black Feminist Critique of Antidiscrimination Doctrine, Feminist Theory and Antiracist Politics," *University of Chicago Legal Forum*, no. 1, article 8 (1989): 139–67.

8 Joycelyn Moody, *Sentimental Confessions: Spiritual Narratives of Nineteenth-Century African American Women* (Athens: University of Georgia Press, 2003), 17.

9 Sondra O'Neale, "Phillis Wheatley," Poetry Foundation, accessed March 12, 2022, https://www.poetryfoundation .org/poets/phillis-wheatley.

10 George Washington to Phillis Wheatley, February 28, 1776, Founders Online, University of Virginia Press, http://founders.archives.gov/ documents/Washington/03-03-02 -0281.

11 Shannon Luders-Manuel, "Jarena Lee: The First Woman African American Autobiographer," JSTOR Daily, December 15, 2018, https:// daily.jstor.org/jarena-lee-the-first -woman-african-american-autobio grapher/.

12 Truth, *Narrative* (1850), 64.

13 James Cone, *The Cross and the Lynching Tree*, paperback ed. (Maryknoll, NY: Orbis, 2013).

14 While some would say this was the *westward expansion* or *manifest destiny*, the history of the United States

suggests *colonization* is a more appropriate term.

15 Barbara Welter, "The Cult of True Womanhood: 1820–1860," *American Quarterly* 18, no. 2 (1966): 151–74, https://doi.org/10.2307/2711179.

16 Elaw, *Memoirs* (1986), 62–63; and Kimberly Blockett, "#sayhername: Recovering Zilpha Elaw's Rebellious Evangelicalism," YouTube video, Harvard Divinity School, May 2, 2018. https://www.youtube.com/watch ?v=fFr6xBhmnWU.

17 Blockett.

18 Thos. K. Doty, introduction to Foote, *Sketch*, 164.

19 W. E. Burghardt Du Bois, "Strivings of the Negro People," *Atlantic*, August 1, 1897, https://www.the atlantic.com/magazine/archive/1897/ 08/strivings-of-the-negro-people/ 305446/. See also W. E. B. Du Bois, *The Souls of Black Folk* (New York: Vintage Books / Library of America, 1990).

20 Washington, *Truth's America*, loc. 473.

21 Foote, *Sketch*, 212. Andrews describes the bush meeting in his footnote at 244n10.

22 Matt 14:13–21; 15:29–39.

23 Elaw, *Memoirs* (1986), 64.

24 Elaw, 66. This could be an allusion to 2 Tim 2:21.

25 Jennifer McFarlane-Harris describes Elaw's introduction as a Pauline address, for instance. Jennifer McFarlane-Harris, "Pauline 'Adoption' Theology as Experiential Performance in the 'Memoirs' of African American Itinerant Preacher Zilpha Elaw," *Performance, Religion, and Spirituality* 2, no. 1 (March 23, 2019): 11, https:// openjournals.utoledo.edu/index .php/prs/article/view/273.

26 Gal 3:28.

27 See Joy R. Bostic, *African American Female Mysticism: Nineteenth-Century Religious Activism* (New York: Palgrave Macmillan, 2013).

Chapter 2: Zilpha Elaw

Portions of this chapter have been published in Kate Hanch, "Zilpha Elaw's Foolish Ministry," *Liturgy* 35, no. 1 (February 2020): 32–37.

1 For a definition of *foolish*, see *Merriam-Webster Dictionary*, s.v. "fool," accessed February 10, 2022, https://www.merriam-webster.com/dictionary/fool.

2 Kimberly Blockett, "Disrupting Print: Emigration, the Press, and Narrative Subjectivity in the British Preaching and Writing of Zilpha Elaw, 1840–1860s," *MELUS* 40, no. 3 (2015): 104, https://doi.org/10.1093/melus/mlv027.

3 All quotes from Elaw in this chapter are derived from her memoir unless noted otherwise.

4 Zilpha Elaw, *Memoirs of the Life, Religious Experience, Ministerial Travels, and Labours of Mrs. Elaw*, ed. and intro. Kimberly D. Blockett (Morgantown: West Virginia University Press, 2021), xvi.

5 1 Cor 2:1, 6.

6 Mary Klages, "Hegemony," in *Key Terms in Literary Theory* (London: Bloomsbury, 2012), 35.

7 William L. Andrews, introduction to *Sisters of the Spirit*, 7.

8 Elaw, *Memoirs* (1986), 53.

9 Elaw, 54.

10 Elaw, 55.

11 Elaw, *Memoirs* (2021), xx. Blockett, following Elaw's language, identifies Rebecca Pierson as Elaw's mistress. The indentured servant type of relationship between them meant that while the Piersons weren't technically her enslavers, they still held power and authority over her.

12 Variations of the hymn are thought to have been written by John Leland, an American Baptist pastor and abolitionist. See R. M. Bishop, ed., *The Christian Hymnal: A Collection of Hymns and Tunes for Congregational and Social Worship* (Cincinnati, OH: H. S. Bosworth, 1882), 247. One version is found in the *Zion's Songster* of 1827. However, other hymnals have alternate wording or have anonymous attributions. Kimberly Blockett, Elaw's biographer, notes that the hymn's variations were found in early Methodist hymnals and could be found anonymously in "older hymnals" such as the *Primitive Christian Hymnal*. Elaw, *Memoirs* (2021), 146n13.

13 Andrews, *Sisters of the Spirit*, 240n4.

14 Elaw, *Memoirs* (1986), 56–57.

15 Elaw, 56–57.

16 Elaw, 57.

17 Bostic writes, "These visitations of ecstatic manifestations and visionary encounters provided meaning and clarity to [nineteenth-century Black women's] lives." Bostic, *African American Female Mysticism*, 48.

18 Elaw, *Memoirs* (1986), 57. This is a reference to Phil 4:7.

19 Elaw, 57–58.

20 Elaw, 61.

21 I am using the King James Version, which is what Elaw would have read from in her ministry.

22 Elaw, *Memoirs* (2021), 146n17.

23 Elaw, 58–59.

24 Elaw, *Memoirs* (1986), 61–63.

25 Elaw, 62.

26 Elaw, 62.

27 Elaw, 84.

28 Elaw, 84.

29 Carroll Smith-Rosenberg, "Cult of Domesticity," in *The Reader's Companion to U.S. Women's History*, ed. Wilma Pearl Mankiller (Boston: Houghton Mifflin, 1998). While this applied to primarily middle- and upper-class white women, its effects permeated the whole of society, including Black women.

30 Elaw, *Memoirs* (1986), 124.

31 Elaw, 136.

32 Elaw, 84–85.

33 For more information on nineteenth century seminaries, see Lucy Townsend, "Anna Peck Sill and the Rise of Women's Collegiate Curriculum" (PhD diss., Loyola University Chicago, 1985).

34 Acts 17:26 KJV; and Elaw, *Memoirs* (1986), 85–86.

35 Elaw, 86–89.

36 Elaw, 83.

37 2 Timothy 4:2 KJV.

38 2 Timothy 4:16 KJV.

39 Elaw, *Memoirs* (1986), 90.

40 Elaw, 91.

41 Blockett, "#sayhername."

42 Elaw, *Memoirs* (1986), 92.

43 John 4:39 KJV.

44 Andrews, *Sisters of the Spirit*, 241n20.

45 Margaret Cullen, "Holy Fire: Biblical Radicalism in the Narratives of Jarena Lee and Zilpha Elaw," in *The Force of Tradition: Response and Resistance in Literature, Religion, and Cultural Studies*, ed. Donald G. Marshall (Lanham, MD: Rowman & Littlefield, 2005), 150.

46 Elaw, *Memoirs* (1986), 66. She describes herself as a "vessel designated for honor."

47 Elaw, 93. The term *connexion*, as used by nineteenth century Methodists, refers to relationships and connections among Methodist churches and more broadly among churches of different denominations. Elaw points to the disconnection between the white and Black churches by mentioning the two distinct "connexions."

48 Elaw, 94–95.

49 Elaw, 96.

50 1 Cor 1:25.

51 Sylvia M. Jacobs, "Nineteenth Century Black Methodist Missionary Bishops in Liberia," *Negro History Bulletin* 44, no. 4 (1981): 83.

52 Elaw, *Memoirs* (1986), 96–97.

53 In historical records, Lady Rogers's name is spelled "Rodgers," but in Elaw's narrative, it appears as "Rogers." She was the wife of Commodore John Rodgers, who "was perhaps the most revered officer of the early American Navy" and served under six US presidents. Rodgers was also an enslaver. Elaw, *Memoirs* (2021), xvi, 140. Lady Lee's husband's family most likely included Robert E. Lee, who would later be a Confederate general in the Civil War. Andrews, *Sisters of the Spirit*, 241n22.

54 Elaw, *Memoirs* (1986), 97.

55 Elaw, 98.

56 In her lecture, Kimberly Blockett suggests Elaw would be more in danger in the Northern states than in Southern states. Blockett, "#sayhername."

57 Elaw, *Memoirs* (1986), 99.

58 Elaw, 128.

59 Elaw, 133–34.

60 Elaw, 104.

61 See Neh 6.

62 Elaw, *Memoirs* (1986), 104.

63 Elaw, 105.

64 See 2 Cor 12:2–3.

65 2 Cor 12:4.

66 Elaw, *Memoirs* (1986), 135.

67 Mitzi Smith suggests Elaw and Old Elizabeth, another nineteenth-century Black woman preacher, both deploy Pauline themes. See Mitzi Smith, "'Unbossed and Unbought': Zilpha Elaw and Old Elizabeth and a Political Discourse of Origins," *Black Theology: An International Journal* 9, no. 3 (2011): 287–311.

68 Elaw, *Memoirs* (1986), 136.

69 Elaw, 137.

70 Elaw, *Memoirs* (2021), 155n92.

71 Elaw, 155n93.

72 Elaw, *Memoirs* (1986), 138.

73 Elaw, 139.

74 Elaw, 138–39.

75 Elaw, *Memoirs* (2021), 107.

76 "I am here" alludes to Isaiah's response when called by God: "Here am I, send me." See Isa 6:8.

77 Elaw, *Memoirs* (1986), 140–41.

78 See 1 Cor 11:7–15; Eph 5:22–24; and 1 Tim 2:9–15.

79 Elaw, *Memoirs* (1986), 148.

80 For more details on what tea meetings looked like, see *The Wesleyan Methodist Association Magazine for 1856*, vol. 19 (London: T. C. Johns, 1856).

81 Elaw, *Memoirs* (1986), 157.

82 Isa 61:1–3. While Elaw cites the King James Version, the most commonly used translation of her day, I am quoting the New Revised Standard Version for readers' ease.

83 Elaw, *Memoirs* (2021), 139, 139n17.

84 H. B. Workman, *Methodism* (Cambridge: Cambridge University Press, 1912), 96–97.

85 Elaw, *Memoirs* (2021), 142.
86 National Archives, "Crime and Punishment," Public Record Office, accessed February 5, 2022, https://www.nationalarchives.gov.uk/education/candp/prevention/g08/g08cs5.htm.
87 Elaw, *Memoirs* (2021), 149.
88 Elaw, *Memoirs* (1986), 155.
89 Elaw, 151.
90 Elaw, 158.
91 Elaw, 160.
92 Kimberly Blockett edited Zilpha Elaw's autobiography, providing information about Elaw after her memoir was written. See her introduction to Elaw, *Memoirs* (2021), xxv–xxvii.
93 Victor Turner, "Betwixt and Between: The Liminal Period in Rites de Passage," in *Reader in Comparative Religion: An Anthropological Approach*, ed. William Armand Lessa, 4th ed. (New York: Harper & Row, 1979), 235.
94 See Nicholas Rescher, *Paradoxes: Their Roots, Range, and Resolution* (Chicago: Open Court, 2001).
95 I put the *em* in *embody* in parenthesis, as I prefer to use the term *bodied* and *bodiment*. We are always bodies; we cannot think without a body.
96 For a fuller treatment, see Sylvester Johnson, *The Myth of Ham in Nineteenth-Century American Christianity: Race, Heathens, and the People of God* (New York: Palgrave Macmillan, 2004).
97 See Ibram X. Kendi, *Stamped from the Beginning: The Definitive History of Racist Ideas in America* (New York: Nation Books, 2016), 177–90.
98 Elaw, *Memoirs* (1986), 105, 131, 147.
99 Blockett, "#sayhername."
100 *Oxford English Dictionary*, s.v. "paradox," accessed May 20, 2022, https://www.oed.com/oed2/00170984;jsessionid=FC156179EC97C952483265CEC1853B2D.
101 Charles L. Campbell and Johan Cilliers, *Preaching Fools: The Gospel as a*

Rhetoric of Folly (Waco, TX: Baylor University Press, 2012), 37.
102 Elaw, *Memoirs* (1986), 92.
103 Campbell and Cilliers, *Preaching Fools*, 30.
104 Campbell and Cilliers, 186.
105 Elaw, *Memoirs* (1986), 92.
106 Harvey Cox, *The Feast of Fools: A Theological Essay on Festivity and Fantasy* (New York: Harper & Row, 1972), 163. Here, he references Leszek Kolakowski, "The Priest and the Jester," *Dissent* 9, no. 3 (Summer 1962): 233.
107 Campbell and Cilliers, *Preaching Fools*, 41.
108 Marion Grau, *Of Divine Economy: Refinancing Redemption* (New York: T&T Clark International, 2004), 3.
109 Elaw, *Memoirs* (1986), 117.
110 Elaw, 118.
111 Kimberly Blockett writes that Elaw's "language is most academic (and sarcastic) when she is being challenged by white men." See Blockett, "Disrupting Print," 103.
112 1 Cor 1:27.
113 Campbell and Cilliers, *Preaching Fools*, 154.
114 Campbell and Cilliers, 154–55.
115 Smith, "Unbossed and Unbought," 292.
116 Elaw, *Memoirs* (1986), 120–21.
117 Elaw, 122.
118 Elaw, 123.
119 See Aja Romano, "Kevin Hart and the Myth of the Internet Mob," *Vox*, December 10, 2018, https://www.vox.com/culture/2018/12/10/18130260/kevin-hart-oscars-homophobic-comedy-backlash-public-shaming-ellen-degeneres.
120 Smith, "Unbossed and Unbought," 308.
121 2 Cor 12:9; and Matt 5:5.
122 Campbell and Cilliers, *Preaching Fools*, 108.
123 Elaw, *Memoirs* (1986), 160.

Chapter 3: Julia Foote

1 Foote, *Sketch*, 4.
2 From the preface to Foote, 4.

3 Margaret Cullen, "Unlikely Pilgrim: The English Journey of Zilpha Elaw,"

International Journal of Religious Tourism and Pilgrimage 1, no. 2 (2009): 37–42.

4 I purposefully use the verb *body* instead of *embody*. The term *embody* developed in the mid-sixteenth century, following the pattern of the Latin *incorporare*, or "to come into the flesh." See *Oxford Dictionary of English*, ed. Angus Stevenson, accessed October 30, 2019, https://www.oxfordreference.com/view/10.1093/acref/9780199571123.001.0001/m_en_gb0262370.

5 M. Shawn Copeland, *Enfleshing Freedom: Body, Race, and Being* (Minneapolis: Fortress, 2010), 8.

6 Recall that chapter 2 also sees the foolishness of God as paradoxical.

7 Ezek 3:1–11. There are some eucharistic implications in this passage. Christians eat the bread (the body of Christ) much like Ezekiel ate the scroll.

8 Ezek 3:9.

9 For more Old Testament examples, see Isa 6:1–8; and Jer 1:4–10.

10 See Isa 40:2–3; Mark 1:2–3; Matt 3:3; Luke 3:4–6; and John 1:23.

11 Matt 3:4.

12 2 Kgs 1:8 NIV.

13 Matt 3:11.

14 Karl Barth, *Church Dogmatics*, vol. 1, pt. 1, trans. and ed. Geoffrey W. Bromiley and Thomas F. Torrance (Edinburgh: T&T Clark, 1975), 111.

15 Barth, 119. As W. Travis McMaken explains, "Revelation itself is the speech and act of God, which is a speech and act that comes ever afresh to humanity and has the character of an event." W. Travis McMaken, *The Sign of the Gospel: Toward an Evangelical Doctrine of Infant Baptism after Karl Barth* (Minneapolis: Fortress, 2013), 75.

16 See Heb 4:12.

17 McMaken, *Sign of the Gospel*, 76.

18 Foote, *Sketch*, 20.

19 Blockett, "Disrupting Print," 109. Sojourner Truth's "Arn't I a Woman" sermon is one such example.

20 Lisa Zimerelli, "The Itinerant Book: Julia A. J. Foote's *A Brand Plucked from the Fire* as a Religious

Activist Text," *Rhetoric Review* 33, no. 2 (2014): 133.

21 Zimerelli, 135.

22 Foote, *Sketch*, 9.

23 Foote, 9–11.

24 Foote, 11.

25 Foote, 11. Black women sometimes named themselves "mother of Israel" or "mother in Israel." This refers to the prophetess Deborah. See, for instance, Virginia Broughton's 1893 speech entitled "Women's Work," delivered to the National Baptist Educational and Foreign Mission Convention in Washington, DC, and published in Laurie F. Maffly-Kipp and Kathryn Lofton, eds., *Women's Work: An Anthology of African-American Women's Historical Writings from Antebellum America to the Harlem Renaissance* (New York: Oxford University Press, 2010), 114. See also Mercedes L. Garcia Bachmann, *Judges* (Collegeville, MN: Liturgical, 2018), 71.

26 Foote, *Sketch*, 11–12.

27 Zimerelli, "Itinerant Book," 137.

28 Richard Allen, *The Life, Experience, and Gospel Labours of the Rt. Rev. Richard Allen* (Philadelphia: Martin & Boden, 1833), Documents of the South, University of North Carolina Chapel Hill, 2000, http://docsouth.unc.edu/neh/allen/menu.html.

29 Zimerelli, "Itinerant Book," 138.

30 Allen, *Life, Experience, and Gospel*, 13–15.

31 Foote, *Sketch*, 14–15.

32 Foote, 15–16.

33 Foote, 171.

34 Her autobiography spells his name with one *t*, while a pamphlet that was distributed (cited below) spells his name as "Van Patten."

35 John F. Van Patten, *The Trial and Life and Confessions of John F. Van Patten Who Was Indicted, Tried and Convicted of the Murder of Mrs. Maria Schermerhorn on the 4th of October Last and Sentenced to Be Executed on the 25th February, 1825* (pamphlet), in *Sabin Americana: History of the Americas, 1500–1926* (New York, 1825), 15.

36 Foote, *Sketch*, 21–23.

37 Zimerelli, "Itinerant Book," 139; see also Robert Wells, *Facing the "King of Terrors": Death and Society in an American Community, 1750–1990* (London: Cambridge University Press, 2000).

38 Zimerelli, "Itinerant Book," 139.

39 John 13:34; and Matt 5:39.

40 Luke 23:34; and Foote, *Sketch*, 22–23.

41 She used the term *dispensation*. The notion of "dispensations" or certain time periods that align with time periods in the Bible is often thought to be anti-Semitic. This was not Foote's intention; nonetheless, it is worth mentioning.

42 Moody, *Sentimental Confessions*, 16.

43 Sheherezade C. Malik and D. Paul Holdsworth, "A Survey of the History of the Death Penalty in the United States," *University of Richmond Law Review* 49, no. 3 (2015): 697.

44 Benjamin Rush, *The Founders' Constitution*, vol. 5, amendment 8, document 16, in *Selected Writings of Benjamin Rush*, ed. Dagobert D. Runes (New York: Philosophical Library, 1947), https://press-pubs .uchicago.edu/founders/documents/ amendVIIIs16.html.

45 Charles Spear, *Essays on the Punishment of Death*, 4th ed. (Boston: C. Spear, 1844), 176.

46 Washington, *Truth's America*, loc. 1499.

47 Foote, *Sketch*, 27–29.

48 Foote, 178.

49 For biblical discussion, see Steven Shaun Tuell, *Reading Nahum-Malachi: A Literary and Theological Commentary* (Macon, GA: Smyth & Helwys, 2016), 179–80.

50 Zech 3:2.

51 Zech 3:7.

52 Zech 3:10.

53 George Whitefield, letter 70, Philadelphia, November 19, 1739, in *Letters of George Whitefield, for the Period 1734–1742* (Edinburgh, Scotland: Banner of Truth Trust, 1976), 77. George Whitefield also advocated for slavery when he converted enslavers.

54 Thorvald E. Källstad, "'A Brand Snatched Out of the Fire': John Wesley's Awareness of Vocation according to the Religio-psychological Theory of Role," *Archive for the Psychology of Religion* 14, no. 1 (1980): 238.

55 John Wesley, *John Wesley's Journal*, ed. Percy Livingstone Parker (Chicago: Moody Press, 1951), 4:90.

56 Jennifer F. McFarlane-Harris, "Autobiographical Theologies: Subjectivity and Religious Language in Spiritual Narratives, Poetry, and Hymnody by African-American Women, 1830–1900" (PhD diss., University of Michigan, 2010), 35.

57 McFarlane-Harris, 35–36.

58 Rev 14:3 KJV.

59 Foote, *Sketch*, 32–34.

60 John Wesley, *The Works of John Wesley*, vol. 5, ed. John Emory (New York: B. Waugh and T. Mason, 1835), 264.

61 Foote, *Sketch*, 43.

62 Foote, 120.

63 Wesley, "A Plain Account of Christian Perfection," in *Works*, 5:263.

64 Foote, *Sketch*, 46–48.

65 Foote, 51.

66 William Cowper, "Light Shining Out of the Darkness," in *Cowper: Verse and Letters*, ed. Brian Spiller (Cambridge, MA: Harvard University Press, 1968), 154.

67 Isa 54:5 KJV.

68 Foote, *Sketch*, 61.

69 Foote, 64.

70 Foote, 95.

71 Foote, 65.

72 Exod 6:30; Jer 1:6; and Isa 6:5.

73 Foote, *Sketch*, 67.

74 Foote, 69–71.

75 Rev 22:1 KJV.

76 Zimerelli, "Itinerant Book," 139–40.

77 Stephen G. Breyer, "A Look Back at the Dred Scott Decision," *Journal of Supreme Court History* 35, no. 2 (2010): 111–12.

78 United States Supreme Court, Roger Brooke Taney, John H. Van Evrie, and Samuel A. Cartwright, *The Dred Scott Decision: Opinion of Chief Justice Taney* (New York: Van Evrie, Horton & Co., 1860), https://www.loc.gov/ item/17001543/.

79 Foote, *Sketch*, 74.

80 Zimerelli, "Itinerant Book," 133.

81 Foote, *Sketch*, 140.

82 Foote, 76–78.

83 Foote, 79–80.

84 Foote, 112–13.

85 With her body, Foote defied what Sarah Ahmed calls a "phenomenology of whiteness"—that is, an inherited habitus affecting how bodies act and move. Whiteness as an inheritance just "is," and this noticed when nonwhite bodies act contrary to its norms or disrupt its schema. Citing Franz Fanon, Ahmed suggests the racialized nonwhite body entering the white space disrupts the habitus of whiteness—the phenomenology of whiteness. The white gaze serves as a reminder that the Black body is not at home. Whiteness is manifest through shared proximity and reified through certain practices and behaviors. See Sara Ahmed, "A Phenomenology of Whiteness," *Feminist Theory* 8, no. 2 (2007): 157. Franz Fanon describes his experience when someone points to him and says, "Look! A Negro." See Frantz Fanon, *Black Skin, White Masks* (New York: Grove, 2008), 93.

86 Foote spells the derogatory term. Given my privilege, I will not.

87 Foote, *Sketch*, 91.

88 Foote, 102.

89 Foote, 102–3.

90 Mark 16:15 KJV.

91 Foote, *Sketch*, 103. Many current biblical scholars see Mark 16:9 and what follows as not a part of the original gospel. However, in Foote's era, people considered this text as Scripture.

92 This feels somewhat similar to Martin Luther's Heidelberg Disputation. Disputation 21 states, "A theology of glory calls evil good and good evil. A theology of the cross calls the thing what it actually is." See "Heidelberg Disputation (1518)," *Book of Concord: The Confessions of the Lutheran Church*, accessed February 14, 2020, https://bookofconcord.org/other -resources/sources-and-context/ heidelberg-disputation/.

93 Zimerelli, "Itinerant Book," 144.

94 Foote, *Sketch*, 104–6.

95 Foote, 105.

96 Foote, 107.

97 Foote, 124.

98 Rom 12:2.

99 Foote, *Sketch*, 120.

100 Elisabeth Schüssler Fiorenza, *The Power of the Word: Scripture and the Rhetoric of Empire* (Minneapolis: Fortress, 2007), 56.

101 Eph 3:20 KJV; and Foote, *Sketch*, 124.

Chapter 4: Sojourner Truth

1 Olive Gilbert, in Sojourner Truth, *Narrative of Sojourner Truth; a Bondswoman of Olden Time, Emancipated by the New York Legislature in the Early Part of the Present Century; with a History of Her Labors and Correspondence Drawn from Her "Book of Life." Also a Memorial Chapter, Giving the Particulars of Her Last Illness and Death*, ed. Olive Gilbert and Frances Titus (Battle Creek, MI: published for author, 1883), 277.

2 See Nell Irvin Painter, *Sojourner Truth: A Life, a Symbol* (New York: W. W. Norton, 1997); and Washington, *Truth's America*. Much of the misconceptions arise from the racist understandings of those who recorded her sermons and speeches. Margaret Washington details the racism by white people in recording Truth's witness in chapter 14 of *Sojourner Truth's America*. I am selective in the stories I relay about her life, attempting to rely on primary sources as much as possible, to show her as a theologian.

3 The term *witness* is not original, though it has been deployed in different ways. In speaking about David Hume and René Descartes's ideas surrounding perception, Alfred

North Whitehead suggests, "Sense-perception of the contemporary world is accompanied by perception of the 'withness' of the body. It is this withness that makes the body the starting point for our knowledge of the circumambient world." See Alfred North Whitehead, *Process and Reality: An Essay in Cosmology*, corrected ed., ed. David Ray Griffin and Donald W. Sherburne (New York: Free Press, 1978), 81. While there is some overlapping of my concept of Truth's "withness" and Whitehead's in relation to bodily experience, that is not the focus of the chapter.

4   Washington describes Sojourner Truth as an African Dutch mystic. Washington, *Truth's America*, loc. 2348.

5   Following her own narrative, this chapter calls Sojourner Truth "Isabella" until she announces her name change.

6   Truth, *Narrative* (1850), 3.

7   Washington, *Truth's America*, loc. 466.

8   Truth, *Narrative* (1850), 59.

9   Truth, 4.

10 Jeroen Dewulf, *The Pinkster King and the King of Kongo: The Forgotten History of America's Dutch-Owned Slaves* (Jackson: University Press of Mississippi, 2017), 6.

11 Washington, *Truth's America*, loc. 868.

12 David N. Gellman, "Pinkster," *Encyclopedia of African American History, 1619–1895: From the Colonial Period to the Age of Frederick Douglass*, ed. Paul Finkelman, Oxford African American Studies Center, accessed November 23, 2019, http://www.oxfordaasc.com.turing.library.northwestern.edu/article/opr/t0004/e0450.

13 Washington, *Truth's America*, loc. 880.

14 Washington, loc. 1259.

15 A carnivalesque theme, complete with a joker, can be found in trickster motifs. The trickster "celebrates" tricking an individual.

16 Bradford Verter, "Interracial Festivity and Power in Antebellum New York:

The Case of Pinkster," *Journal of Urban History* 28, no. 4 (2002): 401.

17 Truth, *Narrative* (1850), 35.

18 Truth, 9–10.

19 Truth, 14.

20 Rom 8:26b.

21 Truth, *Narrative* (1850), 18–19.

22 Truth, 20.

23 The *Narrative* spells his name "Van Wagener," but in the "certificate of character" on the last page of her book, he signs his name as "Van Wagenen." Washington also spells his name as "Van Wagenen."

24 Truth, *Narrative* (1850), 201.

25 Truth, 36.

26 Truth, 35; and Washington, *Truth's America*, loc. 1925.

27 Truth, *Narrative* (1850), 21–22.

28 Truth, 22.

29 Truth, 24–27.

30 Truth, 22.

31 Truth, 25.

32 Truth, 22. "Daguerrian" comes from the daguerreotype, which was an early form of photography used in the 1840s and 1850s. What Gilbert longs for is the technology that is film today.

33 Truth, 49.

34 Truth, 45–46.

35 Truth, 41–45; and Washington, *Truth's America*, loc. 3568.

36 Washington, *Truth's America*, loc. 3269.

37 Truth, 49–50.

38 Truth, 53–55.

39 Truth, 45, 57.

40 Truth, 57.

41 Truth, 59.

42 Luke 10:4.

43 Truth, *Narrative* (1850), 59.

44 Luke 18:25 KJV.

45 Washington, *Truth's America*, loc. 3843.

46 Washington, loc. 3864.

47 Truth, *Narrative* (1850), 68.

48 Gen 3:8 KJV; and Truth, 63–64.

49 Truth, *Narrative* (1850), 73. Gilbert was a white woman, and part of her agenda in recording Truth's *Narrative* was to advocate for the abolition of slavery. Truth seemed to trust her more than other white women who

would record Truth's life and ministry, like Harriet Beecher Stowe and Frances Titus. See Washington, *Truth's America*, loc. 6501, for a larger discussion of Stowe's intentions.

50 Washington, *Truth's America*, loc. 4359–528.

51 Washington, loc. 4630–44. Truth's *Narrative* with the additional "Book of Life" was reprinted in 1875 and edited by Frances Titus. This edition included her "Arn't I a Woman" sermon.

52 Truth, *Narrative* (1850), 73.

53 "Arn't" would have been the word Truth would have used, considering she was from Dutch-speaking New York. I also intentionally choose to evoke the title *sermon* over *speech* because of Sojourner Truth's religious identity as a preacher. Moreover, by utilizing the term *sermon* I attempt to disrupt patriarchal religious thought, which suggests men deliver "sermons" while women give "speeches."

54 Washington, *Truth's America*, loc. 5433–75.

55 Washington, loc. 5475. See also Leslie Podell, "Compare the Speeches," Sojourner Truth Project, accessed March 7, 2022, https://www.the sojournertruthproject.com/compare -the-speeches; and Marius Robinson, "Women's Rights Convention: Sojourner Truth," *Anti-Slavery Bugle* 6 (June 21, 1851): 160, https:// chroniclingamerica.loc.gov/lccn/ sn83035487/1851-06-21/ed-1/seq-4/.

56 Margaret Washington notes that Frances Gage also probably ad-libbed the portion about Truth bearing thirteen children to appeal to white sentimentality. Washington, *Truth's America*, loc. 5458–88.

57 Smith-Rosenberg, "Cult of Domesticity."

58 Washington, *Truth's America*, loc. 6833.

59 Truth, *Narrative* (1883), 134.

60 Truth, 134.

61 Truth, *Narrative* (1850), 12.

62 Truth, *Narrative* (1883), 135.

63 Portions of this discussion were presented at the American Academy of Religion in a paper entitled "Sanctified by the Spirit: Theosis in Jarena Lee, Zilpha Elaw, and Sojourner Truth," San Antonio, TX, November 20, 2016. I thank Michele Watkins for helping me think through concepts relating to deification, Wesleyan pneumatology, and womanist thought.

64 Truth, *Narrative* (1883), 135.

65 Truth, *Narrative* (1850), 18.

66 Truth, *Narrative* (1883), 134.

67 Rom 8:23 KJV.

68 See Judith Butler, "Rethinking Vulnerability and Resistance," in *Vulnerability in Resistance*, ed. Zeynep Gambetti, Leticia Sabsay, and Judith Butler (Durham, NC: Duke University Press, 2016), 12–27.

69 Washington, *Truth's America*, loc. 5355.

70 Jennifer Nash describes vulnerability "as a testament to how we are witnesses to moments when we are subjected to violence, particularly by social structures that have been constructed to discipline and surveil." Jennifer C. Nash, *Black Feminism Reimagined: After Intersectionality* (Durham, NC: Duke University Press, 2019), 119–20.

71 This sermon is recorded in the *New York Tribune*, September 7, 1853, cited in Washington, *Truth's America*, loc. 6107.

72 *National Anti-Slavery Standard*, September 17, 1864.

73 Kelly Oliver, *Witnessing: Beyond Recognition* (Minneapolis: University of Minnesota Press, 2001), 206. Here, Oliver cites Immanuel Levinas's notion of responsibility to the other.

74 Oliver, 206.

75 Truth, *Narrative* (1883), 137–38.

76 In light of twenty-first-century anti-trans legislation for children and adults across the United States, this story is especially dangerous.

77 Washington, *Truth's America*, loc. 6833.

78 Truth, *Narrative* (1883), 139; and Washington, loc. 6840.

79 Psalm 118:6 KJV.

80 Washington, *Truth's America*, loc. 703.

81 Truth, *Narrative* (1850), 69–70.

82 Washington, *Truth's America*, loc. 703.

83 Aaron Powell, *National Anti-Slavery Standard*, May 31, 1955, cited in Washington, loc. 6421, 11227.

84 Truth, *Narrative* (1883), 310.

85 Washington, *Truth's America*, loc. 4116.

86 Washington, loc. 4020.

87 Frederick Douglass, *Narrative of the Life of Frederick Douglass, an American Slave, Written by Himself* (Boston: Anti-Slavery Office, 1845), 117, http://utc.iath.virginia.edu/abolitn/dougnarrhp.html.

88 Truth, *Narrative* (1850), 74.

89 Truth, 74.

90 Washington, *Truth's America*, loc. 6769.

91 Thomas Jefferson, "The Declaration of Independence," 1776, https://www.archives.gov/founding-docs/declaration-transcript.

92 Washington, *Truth's America*, loc. 6777.

93 Washington, loc. 7259–66.

94 Washington, loc. 7740.

95 Colonel John Eaton, quoted in Truth, *Narrative* (1883), 184–85.

96 Truth, *Narrative* (1883), 228. Her narrative describes this incident as recorded in the "Rochester papers" (225).

97 Truth, 228.

98 Ps 139:7 KJV.

Chapter 5: Black Women Preachers as Exemplars of a Prophetic Pastoral Theology

1 Robert R. Wilson, "Prophecy: Biblical Prophecy," in *Encyclopedia of Religion*, 2nd ed., vol. 11, ed. Lindsay Jones (Detroit: Macmillan Reference USA, 2005), 7431.

2 Abraham Joshua Heschel, *The Prophets* (New York: Jewish Publication Society of America, 1962), 5.

3 Gregory the Great, "On the Life of the Pastor," in *The Complete Ante-Nicene and Nicene and Post-Nicene Church Fathers Collection*, ed. Philip Schaff (London: Catholic Way, 2014), loc. 622932, Kindle.

4 John 10:11–18.

5 Howard Thurman, *Mysticism and the Experience of Love* (Wallingford, PA: Pendle Hill, 1961), 4. Joy Bostic also cites this in the opening of her introduction. See Bostic, *African American Female Mysticism*, xi.

6 Elaw, *Memoirs* (1986), 75. Elaw cites Luke 1, when Mary sees the shepherds' awe at Jesus's birth, and reflects upon them inwardly.

7 Foote, *Sketch*, 66.

8 Truth, *Narrative* (1850), 64.

9 Thurman, *Mysticism*, 6.

10 Washington, *Truth's America*, loc. 1514, 2192.

11 Truth, *Narrative* (1850), 26.

12 Elaw, *Memoirs* (1986), 147.

13 Thurman, *Mysticism*, 10.

14 Bostic, *African American Female Mysticism*, 27.

15 Washington, *Truth's America*, loc. 930.

16 For instance, see Washington, *Truth's America*, loc. 2341, 3768, 4950, 8790.

17 Barbara Ann Holmes, *Joy Unspeakable: Contemplative Practices of the Black Church*, 2nd ed. (Minneapolis: Fortress, 2017), 153.

18 Bostic lays out a fuller definition of African American women's mysticism in her book, *African American Female Mysticism*, 44. She cites E. Elonchukwu Uzkwu, *Worship as Body Language: Introduction to Christian Worship: An African Orientation* (Collegeville, MN: Liturgical, 1997), 10.

19 See Bernard McGinn and Edmund Colledge's introduction to *Meister Eckhart: The Essential Sermons, Commentaries, Treatises, and Defense*, trans. Edmund Colledge and Bernard McGinn (New York: Paulist, 1981), 31.

20 Truth, *Narrative* (1850), 36. Bostic emphasizes Truth's declaration as a sign of the apophatic in Bostic, *African American Female Mysticism*, 71–93.

21 Foote, *Sketch*, 34.

22 Foote, 139.

23 Audre Lorde, *Sister Outsider: Essays and Speeches*, rev. ed. (Berkeley, CA: Crossing, 2007), 53.

24 Lorde, 56.

25 Elaw, *Memoirs* (1986), 108–9.

26 Foote, *Sketch*, 175–76.

27 Lorde, *Sister Outsider*, 58.

28 Washington, *Truth's America*, loc. 8053.

29 Washington, loc. 8066.

30 Lorde, *Sister Outsider*, 58.

31 W. T. Dickens, "Frank Conversations: Promoting Peace among the Abrahamic Traditions through Interreligious Dialogue," *Journal of Religious Ethics* 34, no. 3 (2006): 414.

32 Elaw, *Memoirs* (1986), 151.

33 Elaw, 157.

34 Foote, *Sketch*, 81–83.

35 Washington, *Truth's America*, loc. 5636.

36 Rom 8:26.

37 Heb 4:18.

38 Nancy Bedford, "Theological Hermeneutical Spiral," a handout in her introduction to theology class at Garrett-Evangelical Theological Seminary (Evanston, IL, Fall 2013). She demonstrates this process more fully in her "The Most Burning of Lavas: The Bible in Latin America," in *Colonialism and the Bible: Contemporary Reflections from the Global South*, ed. Tat-siong Benny Liew and Fernando F. Segovia, Postcolonial and Decolonial Studies in Religion and Theology (Lanham, MD: Lexington, 2018), 213–31.

39 See chapter 7, entitled "In the Kingdom of Matthias," in Painter, *Sojourner Truth*, 48–61.

40 Phil 1:9–10.

41 Mathilde Roux, "5 Facts about Black Women in the Labor Force," *U.S. Department of Labor Blog*, August 3, 2021, https://blog.dol.gov/2021/08/03/5-facts-about-black-women-in-the-labor-force.

42 "Women of Color in Elective Office 2021," *Center for American Women and Politics*, Eagleton Institute of Politics, Rutgers University, October 30, 2021, https://cawp.rutgers.edu/women-color-elective-office-2021.

43 Amanda Mountain, "Analysis of Race/Ethnicity of United Methodist Clergy—Women by the Numbers," General Commission on the Status and Role of Women: The United Methodist Church, April 2014, https://gcsrw.org/MonitoringHistory/WomenByTheNumbers/tabid/891/post/analysis-of-race-ethnicity-of-united-methodist-clergy/Default.aspx.

44 Kenneth W. Inskeep and John Hessian, *45th Anniversary of the Ordination of Women Executive Summary—Clergy Questionnaire Report 2015*, June 2016, http://download.elca.org/ELCA%20Resource%20Repository/45th_Anniversary_of_the_Ordination_Women_Ordained_Full_Report.pdf?_ga=2.150075382.1511104724.1537455519_676691699.1497547984.

45 Eileen Campbell-Reed, "State of Clergywomen in the United States: A Statistical Update," October 2018, https://eileencampbellreed.org/state-of-clergy/, 8. She cites Courtney Lyons for the Black Baptist statistics in "Breaking through the Extra-Thick Stained-Glass Ceiling: African American Baptist Women in Ministry," *Review and Expositor* 110, no. 1 (Winter 2013): 77–91.

46 Juneteenth is celebrated on June 19 and is the date where emancipation was declared in Texas in 1865.

47 Eboni Marshall Turman, "A Theological Statement from the Black Church on Juneteenth," *Colorlines*, June 19, 2020, https://www.colorlines.com/articles/theological-statement-black-church-juneteenth.

48 Eboni Marshall Turman, "The Black Church Has Always Resisted Anti-Blackness," *Sojourners*, June 24, 2020, https://sojo.net/articles/black-church-has-always-resisted-anti-blackness.

Selected Bibliography

Aimwell, Absalom. "A Pinkster Ode for the Year 1803: Most Respectfully Dedicated to Carolus Africanus, Rex; Thus Rendered in English: King Charles, Captain-general and Commander in Chief of the Pinkster Boys." Early American Imprints. 2nd series, no. 3643. Albany: Printed Solely for the Purchasers and Others, 1803.

Allen, Richard. *The Life, Experience, and Gospel Labours of the Rt. Rev. Richard Allen.* Philadelphia: Martin & Boden, 1833. Documents of the South, University of North Carolina Chapel Hill, 2000. http://docsouth.unc.edu/neh/allen/menu.html.

Andrews, William L., ed. *Sisters of the Spirit: Three Black Women's Autobiographies of the Nineteenth Century.* Bloomington: Indiana University Press, 1986.

Bassard, Katherine Clay. *Spiritual Interrogations: Culture, Gender, and Community in Early African American Women's Writing.* Princeton, NJ: Princeton University Press, 1999.

Bedford, Nancy Elizabeth. *Galatians.* Louisville, KY: Westminster John Knox, 2016.

Blockett, Kimberly. "Disrupting Print: Emigration, the Press, and Narrative Subjectivity in the British Preaching and Writing of Zilpha Elaw, 1840–1860s." *MELUS* 40, no. 3 (2015): 94–109.

———. "#sayhername: Recovering Zilpha Elaw's Rebellious Evangelicalism." YouTube video. Harvard Divinity School, May 2, 2018. https://www.youtube.com/watch?v=fFr6xBhmnWU.

Bostic, Joy R. *African American Female Mysticism: Nineteenth-Century Religious Activism.* New York: Palgrave Macmillan, 2013.

Braxton, Joanne M. "Harriet Jacobs' 'Incidents in the Life of a Slave Girl': The Re-definition of the Slave Narrative Genre." *Massachusetts Review* 27, no. 2 (1986): 379–387.

Brekus, Catherine A. *Strangers & Pilgrims: Female Preaching in America, 1740–1845.* Chapel Hill: University of North Carolina Press, 1998.

Campbell, Charles L., and Johan Cilliers. *Preaching Fools: The Gospel as a Rhetoric of Folly.* Waco, TX: Baylor University Press, 2012.

Campbell-Reed, Eileen. "State of Clergywomen in the United States: A Statistical Update." October 2018. https://eileen campbellreed.org/state-of-clergy/download-state-of-us-clergywomen/.

Chalamet, Christophe, and Hans-Christophe Askani, eds. *The Wisdom and Foolishness of God: First Corinthians 1–2 in Theological Exploration.* Minneapolis: Fortress, 2015.

Cone, James H. *The Cross and the Lynching Tree.* Paperback ed. Maryknoll, NY: Orbis, 2013.

Copeland, M. Shawn. *Enfleshing Freedom: Body, Race, and Being.* Minneapolis: Fortress, 2010.

Cowper, William. *Cowper: Verse and Letters.* Edited by Brian Spillers. Cambridge, MA: Harvard University Press, 1968.

Cox, Harvey. *The Feast of Fools: A Theological Essay on Festivity and Fantasy.* New York: Harper & Row, 1972.

Crenshaw, Kimberlé. "Demarginalizing the Intersection of Race and Sex: A Black Feminist Critique of Antidiscrimination Doctrine, Feminist Theory and Antiracist Politics." *University of Chicago Legal Forum* 1989, no. 1, article 8 (1989): 139–167.

Cullen, Margaret. "Holy Fire: Biblical Radicalism in the Narratives of Jarena Lee and Zilpha Elaw." In *The Force of Tradition: Response and Resistance in Literature, Religion, and Cultural Studies*, edited by Donald G. Marshall. Lanham, MD: Rowman & Littlefield, 2005.

———. "Unlikely Pilgrim: The English Journey of Zilpha Elaw." *International Journal of Religious Tourism and Pilgrimage* 1, no. 2 (2009): 37–42.

Dewulf, Jeroen. *The Pinkster King and the King of Kongo: The Forgotten History of America's Dutch-Owned Slaves.* Jackson: University Press of Mississippi, 2017.

Du Bois, W. E. B. (William Edward Burghardt). *The Souls of Black Folk.* New York: Vintage Books / Library of America, 1990.

———. "Strivings of the Negro People." *Atlantic*, August 1, 1897. https://www.theatlantic.com/magazine/archive/1897/08/strivings-of-the-negro-people/305446/.

Elaw, Zilpha. *Memoirs of the Life, Religious Experience, Ministerial Travels, and Labours of Mrs. Elaw.* 1846. In *Sisters of the Spirit: Three Black Women's Autobiographies of the Nineteenth Century*, edited by William L. Andrews, 49–160. Bloomington: Indiana University Press, 1986.

———. *Memoirs of the Life, Religious Experience, Ministerial Travels, and Labours of Mrs. Elaw.* Edited and introduced by Kimberly D. Blockett. Morgantown: West Virginia University Press, 2021.

Foote, Julia. *A Brand Plucked from the Fire: An Autobiographical Sketch.* New York: George Hughes, 1879.

Goodwin, Mary. "Racial Roots and Religion: An Interview with Howard Thurman." *Christian Century*, May 9, 1973, 533–535.

Grau, Marion. *Of Divine Economy: Refinancing Redemption.* New York: T&T Clark International, 2004.

Grillaert, Nel. "Orthodoxy Regained: The Theological Subtext in Dostoevskij's 'Dream of a Ridiculous Man.'" *Russian Literature* 62, no. 2 (2007): 155–173. https://doi.org/10.1016/j.ruslit.2007.08.002.

Hanch, Kate. "Voices of Authority and Theological Method: Who We Read Is Just as Important as What We Read." May 27, 2014. https://nearemmaus.wordpress.com/2014/05/27/voices-of-authority-and-theological-method-who-we-read-is-just-as-important-as-what-we-read/.

Hessian, John, and Kenneth Inskeep. "45th Anniversary of the Ordination of Women: Church Setting Experiences—Clergy Qualitative Report." Research and Evaluation, Office of the Presiding Bishop of the Evangelical Lutheran Church in America. ELCA Archives, December 2016. http://download.elca.org/ELCA%20Resource%20Repository/45th AnniversaryExperiencesQualwAppendix.pdf.

Hodges, Graham Russell Gao. "Trickster." *Encyclopedia of African American History, 1619–1895: From the Colonial Period to the Age of Frederick Douglass.* Edited by Paul Finkelman. New York: Oxford University Press, 2008. Oxford African American Studies Center. http://www.oxfordaasc.com.turing.library.northwestern.edu/article/opr/t0004/e0561.

Holmes, Barbara Ann. *Joy Unspeakable: Contemplative Practices of the Black Church.* 2nd ed. Minneapolis: Fortress, 2017.

Jacobs, Sylvia M. "Nineteenth Century Black Methodist Missionary Bishops in Liberia." *Negro History Bulletin* 44, no. 4 (1981): 83–93.

Johnson, Sylvester A. *The Myth of Ham in Nineteenth-Century American Christianity: Race, Heathens, and the People of God.* New York: Palgrave Macmillan, 2004.

Källstad, Thorvald E. "'A Brand Snatched Out of the Fire': John Wesley's Awareness of Vocation according to the Religio-psychological Theory of Role." *Archive for the Psychology of Religion* 14, no. 1 (1980): 237–245.

Kirk-Duggan, Cheryl A. *Refiner's Fire: A Religious Engagement with Violence.* Minneapolis: Fortress, 2001.

Klages, Mary. *Key Terms in Literary Theory.* London: Bloomsbury, 2012.

Lorde, Audre. *Sister Outsider: Essays and Speeches.* Revised ed. Berkeley, CA: Crossing, 2007.

Luders-Manuel, Shannon. "Jarena Lee: The First Woman African American Autobiographer." JSTOR Daily, December 15, 2018. https://daily.jstor.org/jarena-lee-the-first-woman-african-american-autobiographer/.

Maddox, Randy L. *Responsible Grace: John Wesley's Practical Theology.* Nashville: Kingswood, 1994.

Maffly-Kipp, Laurie F., and Kathryn Lofton, eds. *Women's Work: An Anthology of African-American Women's Historical Writings from Antebellum America to the Harlem Renaissance.* New York: Oxford University Press, 2010.

Malik, Sheherezade C., and D. Paul Holdsworth. "A Survey of the History of the Death Penalty in the United States." *University of Richmond Law Review* 49, no. 3 (2015): 693–710.

McFarlane-Harris, Jennifer. "Pauline 'Adoption' Theology as Experiential Performance in the 'Memoirs' of African American Itinerant Preacher Zilpha Elaw." *Performance, Religion, and Spirituality* 2, no. 1 (March 23, 2019): 9–33. https://openjournals.utoledo.edu/index.php/prs/article/view/273.

McFarlane-Harris, Jennifer F. "Autobiographical Theologies: Subjectivity and Religious Language in Spiritual Narratives, Poetry, and Hymnody by African-American Women, 1830–1900." PhD diss., University of Michigan, 2010.

Moody, Joycelyn. *Sentimental Confessions: Spiritual Narratives of Nineteenth-Century African American Women.* Athens: University of Georgia Press, 2003.

Mountain, Amanda. "Analysis of Race/Ethnicity of United Methodist Clergy—Women by the Numbers." General Commission on the Status and Role of Women: The United Methodist Church. April 2014. https://gcsrw.org/MonitoringHistory/

WomenByTheNumbers/tabid/891/post/analysis-of-race
-ethnicity-of-united-methodist-clergy/Default.aspx.

Nash, Jennifer C. *Black Feminism Reimagined: After Intersectionality*. Durham, NC: Duke University Press, 2019.

O'Neale, Sondra. "Phillis Wheatley." Poetry Foundation. Accessed March 12, 2022. https://www.poetryfoundation.org/poets/phillis-wheatley.

Phan, Peter C., and Jung Young Lee. *Journeys at the Margin: Toward an Autobiographical Theology in American-Asian Perspective*. Collegeville, MN: Liturgical, 1999.

Podell, Leslie. "Compare the Speeches." Sojourner Truth Project. Accessed March 7, 2022. https://www.thesojournertruthproject.com/compare-the-speeches.

Public Record Office. "Crime and Punishment." Accessed February 5, 2022. https://www.nationalarchives.gov.uk/education/candp/prevention/g08/g08cs5.htm.

Robinson, Marius. "Women's Rights Convention: Sojourner Truth." *Anti-Slavery Bugle* 6 (June 21, 1851). https://chroniclingamerica.loc.gov/lccn/sn83035487/issues/1851/.

Roux, Mathilde. "5 Facts about Black Women in the Labor Force." *U.S. Department of Labor Blog*, August 3, 2021. https://blog.dol.gov/2021/08/03/5-facts-about-black-women-in-the-labor-force.

Rutgers Eagleton Institute for Politics. "Women of Color in Elective Office 2021." Center for American Women in Politics. Accessed October 30, 2021. https://cawp.rutgers.edu/women-color-elective-office-2021.

Rutledge, John. "Paynter Views CBF as a 'Denominetwork.'" *Baptist Standard*, June 27, 2014. https://www.baptiststandard.com/news/baptists/paynter-views-cbf-as-a-denominetwork/.

Teel, Karen. *Racism and the Image of God*. New York: Palgrave Macmillan, 2010.

Townsend, Lucy. "Anna Peck Sill and the Rise of Women's Collegiate Curriculum." PhD diss., Loyola University Chicago, 1985.

Truth, Sojourner. *Narrative of Sojourner Truth; a Bondswoman of Olden Time, Emancipated by the New York Legislature in the*

Early Part of the Present Century; with a History of Her Labors and Correspondence Drawn from Her "Book of Life." Also a Memorial Chapter, Giving the Particulars of Her Last Illness and Death. Compiled by Olive Gilbert and Frances W. Titus. Battle Creek, MI: published for author, 1883.

———. *Narrative of Sojourner Truth.* Compiled by Olive Gilbert. Boston: published for author, 1850. Kindle.

Tuell, Steven Shawn. *Reading Nahum-Malachi: A Literary and Theological Commentary.* Macon, GA: Smyth & Helwys, 2016.

Turman, Eboni Marshall. "The Black Church Has Always Resisted Anti-Blackness." *Sojourner,* June 24, 2020. https://sojo.net/articles/black-church-has-always-resisted-anti-blackness.

———. "A Theological Statement from the Black Church on Juneteenth." *Colorlines,* June 19, 2020. https://www.colorlines.com/articles/theological-statement-black-church-juneteenth.

Van Patten, John F., and New York Court of Oyer and Terminer. *The Trial and Life and Confessions of John F. Van Patten Who Was Indicted, Tried and Convicted of the Murder of Mrs. Maria Schermerhorn on the 4th of October Last and Sentenced to Be Executed on the 25th February, 1825.* Pamphlet. In *Sabin Americana: History of the Americas, 1500–1926.* New York, 1825. link.gale.com/apps/doc/CY0109638528/SABN?u=northwestern&sid=bookmark-SABN&xid=05e236eb&pg=1.

Washington, George, to Phillis Wheatley, February 28, 1776. Founders Online. University of Virginia Press. http://founders.archives.gov/documents/Washington/03-03-02-0281.

Washington, Margaret. *Sojourner Truth's America.* Urbana: University of Illinois Press, 2009. Kindle.

Welter, Barbara. "The Cult of True Womanhood: 1820–1860." *American Quarterly* 18, no. 2 (1966): 151–174. https://doi.org/10.2307/2711179.

Wesley, John. "A Plain Account of Christian Perfection." In *The Works of John Wesley,* 1872. Reprint, Grand Rapids, MI: Zondervan, 1958–1959.

Wesleyan Methodist Association Magazine for 1856. Vol. 19. London: T. C. Johns, 1856.

Whitefield, George. *Letters of George Whitefield, for the Period 1734–1742*. Edinburgh, Scotland: Banner of Truth Trust, 1976.

Workman, Herbert B. *Methodism*. Cambridge: Cambridge University Press, 1912.

Index of Names
and Subjects

abolition, x, 7, 9, 14, 46, 51, 85,
    100, 131, 133–34, 140, 161
abolitionist. *See* abolition
Allen, Richard, 76–79, 84, 105,
    160
angel, 2, 21, 86, 95–97, 153

Barth, Karl, 74
Bedford, Nancy, 163
Bible, x, 2, 7, 25–26, 37, 42, 46,
    53, 55, 59, 72, 75, 80–81,
    89–90, 96, 110, 113, 124, 127,
    131–32, 161
Blackness, 4, 11, 18, 59, 115, 139
Blockett, Kimberly, 18, 57

body (bodying, bodiliness, as a noun
    and verb), 3–4, 18, 40, 44, 50,
    57–58, 70–76, 78–80, 82–83,
    85, 90, 95–98, 100, 103–4,
    106, 108–10, 112, 115, 122,
    127–28, 132, 136–39, 147,
    149–51, 154–59
brand, 69, 85–91, 97

camp meeting, 12–14, 22, 56, 141
Christ, 2, 15, 22, 24–25, 35–37,
    50–51, 56, 68, 72–75, 77, 81,
    85, 96–97, 100, 104, 107,
    108–9, 135, 137, 151–52, 160,
    162

Civil War, viii, 8–11, 84, 88, 99, 138, 146–57, 158
code-switching, 59
colonization, 9, 57, 59, 99
Cone, James, 8
contemplation, 3–5, 12, 15, 66–67, 150–55
Copeland, M. Shawn, 71
Cowper, William, 93
Cox, Harvey, 61
Crenshaw, Kimberlé, 5
cult of domesticity, 9–10, 28, 135

death penalty, 82–85
deification, 121, 132
Douglass, Frederick, 3, 46, 139, 142–43
Dred Scott v. Sandford, 11, 98–100, 110, 144–45
Du Bois, W. E. B., 10

Eckhart, Meister, 155
Elaw, Zilpha, x, xi–xiii, 1–2, 4–5, 7–15, 17–68, 70, 80, 138, 149–52, 154–56, 159–60, 162–63
empathy, 3, 137, 150, 159–62
erotic, 115, 139, 155–56, 158
evangelist, x, 10–11, 17, 28, 48, 56, 58–59, 87, 104

finitude, 154
fool, 17–21, 23–25, 27–28, 32, 34–36, 38, 44–45, 50, 52–53, 55–64, 66–68, 86, 94, 149
foolishness. *See* fool

Foote, Julia, 2, 4–5, 7–15, 69–110, 144, 149–52, 154–55, 157, 159–66

Gage, Frances, 134
Garrison, William Lloyd, 46, 133
Ghost, Holy. *See* Spirit, Holy
Gilbert, Olive, 111, 125, 133, 141, 143
Gregory the Great, 151

Ham, curse of, 58–59
Heschel, Abraham, 149–50
hope, 3, 30, 37, 56, 62–64, 66, 70, 85, 100, 102, 108, 117, 142, 161
humor, 67, 142–46

image (of God), 5, 104, 139, 147, 151, 155, 165
imago Dei. *See* image (of God)
incarnate. *See* incarnation
incarnation, 50, 72, 74, 85, 109–10, 121, 162
interruptive, 64–67
Isabella. *See* Truth, Sojourner
Isaiah (prophet), 37, 46, 53–54, 73, 94–95, 102
itinerancy, 1, 11, 13–14, 19, 23, 31–32, 45, 62, 64, 68, 87, 95–96, 98, 100, 104–6, 133, 160
itinerant. *See* itinerancy

Jeremiah, 45–46, 95
Jesus, 1–3, 8, 12–15, 19, 22–24, 33–34, 36–37, 40–41, 43, 50, 54, 60, 62, 64, 67, 72–74, 80,

82–83, 87, 91, 101–2, 106,
113, 121–22, 125, 129–30,
137, 151, 162
joy, 22–23, 80, 95, 115, 122,
141–42

Lee, Jarena, 6
liminal, 28, 58–61, 66–68
Lorde, Audre, 155–59
love, 2, 4–5, 8, 15, 20, 22–26, 30,
55, 66, 70, 79, 81, 83, 90,
92–95, 109, 113, 115, 117,
121–23, 132–33, 137, 139,
147, 149, 151, 158, 160,
163–64, 166
lynching, 8, 84

marriage, 2, 25–30, 57, 76, 91–98,
118
Matthias, kingdom of, 128–29
McFarlane-Harris, Jennifer, 14, 88
Methodism, 2, 7, 13–14, 19–21,
23–25, 32, 34, 41, 49, 51–52,
54, 57, 66, 70, 76–79, 85–89,
92, 99–100, 105–6, 115, 125,
127–28, 154, 160, 163–64
Moody, Jocelyn, 6, 83
Moses, 46, 72, 95, 121
motherhood, 20, 47, 76–77, 79–80,
89, 112–13, 116–17, 124,
126–27, 135, 140, 152, 154,
157, 163
mystical. See mysticism
mysticism, 3–5, 12, 15, 21–24,
38, 44, 89, 95, 112, 121–22,
150–55

Northampton (commune), 131–33,
134

Oliver, Kelly, 139

Painter, Nell Irvin, 163
paradox, 18, 35, 58, 60–62, 66, 68
pastoral, 6, 9, 149–51, 157, 159,
161–62, 165
Paul, apostle, 4, 14, 18–19, 23–24,
28–29, 33, 35, 38, 40, 44, 50,
60–61, 64, 67, 69, 101, 103,
118, 137, 162–63
perfection, 90, 109
Pinkster, 113–17, 120
pneumatology, 8, 52, 67, 122
police, 54–55, 59, 165–66
power, viii, 10, 18–19, 28, 30,
35–39, 39, 42–43, 50, 60,
64, 66, 67–68, 70, 91, 93,
105, 109–12, 121, 123–24,
136, 143, 145–49, 155–56,
158
prophetic, 7, 9, 17, 21, 33, 37, 50,
66, 70, 72–74, 78–79, 86, 94,
97, 121, 150–51, 159, 162
punching up, 66–67

Quakers, 13, 14, 20, 31, 37, 51,
119, 124, 153–54

resistance, 15, 42, 50, 55, 94–95,
100, 103–5, 137, 141, 152,
166
rhetoric, 10, 35, 59, 63, 75, 100,
109, 134
Rush, Benjamin, 84

Sabbath, 48
salvation, 5, 33, 55, 73–74, 81, 88,
95, 108, 115

sanctification, 4, 8, 13, 67, 71, 89–95, 98, 101–2, 108, 132, 152, 163

Scripture, 7–8, 15, 17, 29, 37, 43, 51, 54, 67, 70, 72, 74–75, 78, 80–83, 85–86, 89, 90, 100–102, 106, 108–10, 122, 131–32, 136–37, 150, 155, 166

Second Great Awakening, 12, 48, 88

sermon, 34–36, 38–39, 41–42, 50, 53, 56–57, 71, 106–8, 110, 131, 134–38, 149–51, 156, 158

sexism, 5, 52, 151, 164

slavery, 4, 7, 11, 34, 39–40, 46, 49–50, 59, 77, 88, 99, 119, 133–34, 136, 140, 143, 153–54, 162–63

Smith, Mitzi, 67

Spirit, Holy, 3, 7, 20, 22, 24, 29, 37–38, 52–53, 67, 74, 77, 96, 97, 101, 106, 112–15, 118–19, 122, 124, 127, 129, 133, 137, 141–42, 145, 147, 163

street car, 147–48

Supreme Court, 11, 98, 144–45

Taney, Roger, 98–100

Thurman, Howard, 151–54

trickster, 62–63, 66

Trinity, 24, 149, 163

Turman, Eboni Marshall, 166

Truth, Sojourner, 3–5, 7–15, 84, 111–55, 159–66

Van Patten, John, 79, 81–85

vision, 2, 5, 22–23, 44–45, 48, 68, 72, 86, 95, 97–98, 107, 112, 120–22, 128, 130, 137, 152–53, 155

vulnerability, 36, 137, 162

Washington, Margaret, 133

Wesley, John, 49, 51–52, 54, 87–90, 109, 132

Wheatley, Phillis, 6

whiteness, 106, 154

white supremacy, 5, 7, 13, 70, 99, 113, 137, 139, 147, 150, 166

Whitfield, George, 87–88

withness, xiii, 111–15, 122–26, 128–32, 134, 136–39, 141, 145–48, 149, 162, 178–79

witness, 3, 8, 13, 28, 33, 50, 55, 67, 74, 76, 81, 109, 112, 122, 131–32, 136, 139–40, 148, 164, 166

word, 55, 70–75, 78, 80, 85, 89, 91, 95–96, 100, 102, 104, 106–10, 149–51

Zimerelli, Lisa, 106

Index of Bible Passages

Genesis

1	10
2:2–3	132
12:1	47
15	72

Exodus

2:22	46
21:23	82
24	72

Deuteronomy

19:21	82

1 Kings

1:8	73

Nehemiah

2–13	42–43

Job

3	40

Psalms

104	47
118:6	141
139	121

Isaiah
40	73
54	94
61	53

Jeremiah
1:7	45

Ezekiel
3	72–73

Joel
2	103, 107–8

Jonah
1	2

Micah
4:13	107

Zechariah
3	86–87, 97
7:11	143

Matthew
3:11	74
3:20	73

Mark
16:15	106

Luke
4	54,
15	56,
18:25	130

John
1:4	72
4	36

Acts
2	101

Romans
8:23	137
16:3	103

1 Corinthians
1:18	18
1:23	50
1:27	35
11:9	26
12:13	24

Galatians
3:20	14–15

Ephesians
4:13	42
6:17	108

Philippians
1:9	163

1 Timothy
2	103

Hebrews
4:3	70
13	51

1 John
4:18	133

Revelation
21–22	97